# LIVING BY FAITH

## ...Pleasing God

This book answers the question,
"How do I acquire faith?"

by

## A Satisfied Layman

We live by faith, not by sight. 2 Cor. 5:7

Without faith it is impossible to please God. Heb. 11:6

**Word Resources, Inc.**
Portland, Oregon

This book is available in free downloadable format and
LARGE PRINT type at **www.tetragrammaton.org**
(Please see the back pages for information regarding this web site.)

**This book is not copyrighted.**

It may be copied and reproduced without restriction.

**Word Resources, Inc.**
P.O. Box 301294
Portland, Oregon 97294-9294

Published in 2001

Released for World Wide Web distribution in 2001

ISBN 0-9703890-2-7

# CONTENTS

OVERVIEW:

SECTION 1: **Living by Faith**

SECTION 2: **Practical Issues in Faith**

Because you love Jesus, you want your faith to please Him now. In Heaven, you will also want to look back on a life that was lived by faith.

*Must you wait until your first meeting with Jesus before you can know if He was satisfied with your faith?*

•

This book attempts to define faith. It also attempts to show you how to live by faith in your contemporary world. Most of all, this book tries to answer the question, "How does a believer acquire faith?"

Can *you* say that you have as much faith as God wants you to have today? In Chapter 5 you will see the joy of the believer who can say, "Thank you Jesus for giving me faith that totally satisfies you."

•

No book has all of the answers, and that is certainly true of this one. You will be reading about faith as understood and experienced by only one, imperfect believer. Scripture shows the believer how to acquire faith. Yet, each believer also has unique strengths and weaknesses. After carefully considering Scripture, allow God to independently lead you as you grow in faith. Learn from this book if it is helpful, but *do not depend on it to produce your faith.*

•

Living by faith is costly. If you begin to truly live by faith, you will someday look back and realize that the joy of living by faith was commensurate to the cost of pursuing faith. A growing faith will be a direct result of the adversity you are willing to encounter for it. (Simply stated, learning to live by faith is a process of transferring your trust from yourself and your society to Jesus. Learning to rely less on your own ability in order to trust Him is difficult.)

•

This book was written anonymously so that it would not attract attention to any individual. Nonetheless, portions of the text have been written in the first person because the outworking of faith requires the application of biblical truth to personal experience. You may gain understanding by seeing me groping for answers and even failing. As you will see later in the book, I believe faith is best taught by *modeling* it for other believers.  In order for me to model faith, you must see my thought processes and struggles.

Finally, in some small degree, I want to be a "witness" advocating the positive results of living by faith.  That recommendation comes from my own experience of asking God to give me faith while working in the electrical trade for the past 20 years.  It reflects my awareness that God is answering my prayer for faith  by allowing me to progressively lose a 35-year battle with diabetes.  This includes an unknown future in light of mental and emotional deterioration resulting from two episodes of extremely low blood sugar levels in the last two years.  In my mid-50s I lost my pension as the result of a plant closure.  I have since been unemployed twice.  Living by faith—that is, learning to trust Jesus—is becoming increasingly costly for me.  Nonetheless, I continue to pursue faith aggressively.  I would not choose to live any other way.

After personally experiencing some of both its cost and benefits, I wholeheartedly recommend that you pursue faith.

•

This book is divided into two sections.  Section 1 explains the process of acquiring faith.  Section 2 contains shorter chapters related to living by faith.

The illustrations in the first seven chapters portray a high degree of commitment and cost.  These illustrations are often qualified in Section 2.  As you read, simply be aware that further explanations are yet to come.  For example:

In the first two chapters, you will see illustrations of individuals investing a substantial portion of retirement funds in ministry, sacrificing a career in order to spend more time in prayer, or foregoing certain medications or physician's care in favor of trusting Jesus.  These are legitimate illustrations that have come from the lives of real believers.   Nonetheless, these decisions were prayerfully balanced with the caution given in Chapter 22 to avoid self-inflicted suffering.  Don't use these illustrations as general models of faith.  God will lead you individually as you learn to trust Him.  You should never try to mimic someone else's faith.

*Faith does not replace appropriate planning and decision-making.  God has given us sound judgment as a tool to be used in personal finances, healthful living, and the like.  Faith is not a fatalistic approach to life.  Nor does faith ignore either human wisdom or beneficial social institutions.  In specific instances, however, God may lead us to go beyond trusting mere human effort.*

# SECTION 1

## LIVING BY FAITH

Faith must first be defined because you must know what faith is before you can pursue it. Next, you must determine whether faith is optional for some believers, or if God expects it of you also. It will then be helpful for you to understand how growing faith operates before you proceed to acquire faith for yourself. At some point, you will need to ask yourself the question, "Why should I want faith?" Section 1 concludes with some practical advice concerning pursuing faith.

# 1 What is Acting Faith?

**D**o you want to live an active and effective life of faith? Do you want your faith to please God?

We often identify faith with one of two extremes. The first extreme is a faith that produces little more than random "blessings." The second extreme identifies faith with miracles and flamboyant public displays of healing.

But what does it mean to *live* by faith? Can the average Christian today live by faith in the same way that the believers did in the book of Acts?

Yes! Jesus died and rose again so that we might have that kind of faith in our daily lives—and that we as His children might know the exhilaration of a faith that pleases God.

But it will be costly.

## Faith found in the New Testament

The New Testament uses the word *faith* as both an *action* (with the meaning of the verb *to trust*) and as an object—something a believer possesses (having the sense of a noun).

The Canaanite woman in Matthew 15:21-28 acted by faith when she asked Jesus to heal her daughter. She placed herself in a vulnerable position because she believed Jesus could help. After testing her commitment to act in faith, Jesus said in verse 28, "Woman, you have great faith! Your request is granted." And her daughter was immediately healed.

The Canaanite woman's faith was expressed in action; she *trusted* Jesus to *do* something that was very important to her.

Scripture also uses the word *faith* in the sense of a noun. In Acts 6:7, Luke reported that "...the word of God spread...and a large number of priests became obedient to the faith." In contrast, Paul told Timothy in 1 Timothy 4:1 that "In later times some will abandon the faith."

The Greek word *pistis*—which is translated into English as *faith*—appears 241 times in the New Testament. Yet, it is used infrequently in its noun sense. It is not possible to precisely count the number of times the word *faith* is used as a noun in either the Greek or English New Testaments. Sometimes it could have either sense. However, of the 241 times the word *faith* appears in the New Testament, it is probably used only 20 or 30 times as a noun.

The faith described in the New Testament is primarily that of men and women who were trusting Jesus. Their life displayed the *action* of faith. They trusted Jesus when they took the first risky step of meeting in the Temple as Messianic Jews. They trusted Him when they were driven out of Jerusalem in the first wave of persecution. They trusted Him when they dared to proclaim the Gospel to Gentiles. And they trusted Him when they were taken to the arena as martyrs.

### Does a *verb* or a *noun* best represent your faith?

How do you characterize your own faith? Is your faith expressed by action? Are you frequently in situations in which you trust Jesus for the outcome of important decisions or events in your life?

Or is your faith primarily something you possess; the doctrines you believe? Do you rarely dependent on Jesus for His guidance in difficult events in your life?

### Faith in action

The account of the centurion stationed in Capernaum gives an interesting example of faith (Matthew 8:5-9). The centurion sent messengers to Jesus asking that his servant be healed. Jesus answered that He would go to the centurion's house.

The centurion then made his surprising reply through friends that he was unworthy to have Jesus come into his house, but that he knew Jesus could "just say the word" and the servant would be healed. (Luke 7:1-10 indicates that the centurion did not consider himself worthy to go to Jesus in person.) Jesus marveled at the centurion's response saying, "I tell you the truth, I have not found anyone in Israel with such great faith." Jesus then told the centurion's representatives, "'Go! It will be done just as [the centurion] believed it would.' And his servant was healed at that very hour."

Why did the centurion's rather cumbersome elaboration so please Jesus when he said, "For I myself am a man under authority, with soldiers under me. I tell this one, 'Go,' and he goes; and that one 'Come,' and he comes. I say to my servant, 'Do this,' and he does it"?

The centurion understood two important components of faith.

First, he understood the nature of authority. He was in the middle of a military chain of command; he had superiors over him and he obeyed their orders. He also had subordinates under him who obeyed his commands. So when the centurion saw the extreme physical need of his servant, he understood how authority could be used to alleviate the servant's suffering. Secondly, he understood by faith that Jesus was *the* authority who could deliver his servant from this physical bondage.

The centurion's faith was not an expression of emotional frenzy. Rather, he understood what needed to transpire in order for his servant to be healed, and he had total confidence that Jesus had the authority to heal. Social amenities or curiosity concerning Jesus' healing technique were inconsequential to his servant's need. The issue was simply Jesus' authority.

That is faith!

## True faith involves risk

Both the Canaanite woman and the centurion took a risk when they came to Jesus. She was a Gentile and knew that she risked rebuff by talking to a Jew. Further, Jesus initially ignored the woman's plea for her daughter. Jesus purposely made it difficult for her to make her request. He did not quickly or privately answer her entreaty. Rather, He brought her to a point of full and public commitment of her will before He healed her daughter. Jesus did not allow her to be casual with Him. He forced her to declare her need of His help in front of her acquaintances and neighbors.

She took a great risk. What if this itinerant Jew could not help her after she had humiliated herself before the whole town?

The centurion also took a risk. He was a career soldier who was aware of protocol. The Roman military was an important means of advancement in Roman society. Asking Jesus to heal his slave was a departure from his peers' expectations. The centurion greatly increased his personal risk by publicly expressing confidence in Jesus' authority to heal. He made a full commitment of faith rather than making a perfunctory request in behalf of his servant. What if Jesus would not help?

As you read further, you will see an emphasis in this book on taking risks while developing faith. J. Hudson Taylor, who founded the China Inland Mission (now the Overseas Missionary Fellowship), decided to go through medical training in England without financial assistance from either his father or the mission to which he had applied. (His father and the mission each thought the other was providing for Taylor's expenses, and he deliberately did not tell either of them otherwise.) He reasoned that he would need to live by faith in China and should begin practicing during his student years. His biography chronicles a life that continued to demonstrate his great trust in God for personal survival and ministry. Consider this statement by Taylor:

> Unless there is an element of risk in your exploits for God, there is no need for faith.

## Faith defined

Because faith may be applied differently in each circumstance, I am using three overlapping definitions. These three definitions are:

1. Faith is trusting God (Jesus) rather than relying on conventional means for something you need.
2. Faith is trusting God (Jesus) for an outcome even when that trust incurs personal risk which could otherwise be avoided.
3. Faith is trusting God (Jesus) for an outcome which is impossible through human effort irrespective of the willingness to incur risk.

**1. *Faith is trusting God (Jesus) rather than relying on conventional means for something you need.*** In each of the three definitions, the Person of God is always the object of faith. This trust is always directed toward God (the Godhead corporately), or the Father, Jesus, or the Spirit. Thus, it is not a generalized hope that things will mysteriously improve. It is always direct reliance on the divine Person. We are not trusting in our religious faith. We are not trusting in a vague Providence or ill-defined Higher Power. Biblical faith is a reliance on the God of the Bible and in His personal care and provision for us.

Furthermore, faith is trusting God rather than something else. In almost all cases, our trust will be diverted from those things that other people in the same circumstances would normally trust. The object of *normal* trust is what I call *conventional means*.

For example, we could say that for J. Hudson Taylor, conventional means of attending medical school in England during the early 1850s would certainly include allowing a parent or a mission to provide financial assistance. There was nothing wrong with that kind of help. However, Taylor felt led to trust God for his income rather than to accept the same provisions that other Christians in like circumstances might appropriately have used.

You can see the conflict I have introduced. I am not saying that there is anything wrong with conventional means. Though each case must be considered individually, using conventional means is the normal way to live in society. However, as an act of faith, God may lead us to trust Him alone for something rather than depending upon means society normally provides for that purpose.

*It is important that you understand my intent in suggesting that faith does not rely on conventional means.* No one—believer or otherwise—could live without relying on society's provisions. We work to earn money, we use money to purchase food, and so forth. Faith may be fully exercised in any of these steps. We do not sit down to a bare table and demand that God miraculously supply an abundant meal so we can prove that we live by faith. In almost all cases of God's provision through faith, He will use elements of conventional means as the supply channel.

At the same time, God may—at His discretion—remove one or two elements of conventional means from a chain of events through which we would normally expect provision. In these single elements, He may direct us to trust Him rather than the ordinary, expected avenues of supply. I am not suggesting that faith supplants all use of conventional means. I am merely suggesting that, in certain instances, God may guide us to trust Him directly to provide for those needs rather than to trust in the normal means of provision.

There is, however, a more subtle distinction between trusting God and trusting conventional means. The issue has to do with that which we view as our *primary recourse* for a given need. If I have sought God's help and direction in meeting an unexpected financial obligation and He directs me to draw the needed funds from a savings account, I am placing my trust in God rather than conventional means because He has become my primary recourse. On the other hand, if I merely use the saving account without first seeking God's provision or direction, I am not acting by faith, but am depending on conventional means. In this second instance, my savings account has become my primary recourse. Someone may object, saying that this distinction is merely one of definition. That is the very nature of faith. In this illustration, my degree of faith has little to do with the ultimate source of the money I use for payment. My degree of faith has everything to do with whether or not I turn first to God as my primary recourse, asking Him to meet my need. If I seek Him first, i t is His prerogative to provide for me. He may do that through an established saving account or through any other means He chooses.

The same distinction could be made in using medicine as a primary recourse during illness as against turning first to God in faith. The same would be true of any other area in which our society provides legitimate aid. I am not saying that all we must do is repeat a prayer and then go ahead with our initial plan. God knows the integrity of our heart. He will provide for us if we will come to Him in faith. But He will not allow us to use Him merely to accomplish our own ends.

Though *risk* is not mentioned in this first definition, the element of risk is obvious. Trusting God in place of anything else that is more familiar to us will be perceived as being less reliable.

This definition of faith has introduced many issues requiring explanation. By the end of the book I will attempt to resolve some of these issues. For now, however, you should realize that the life of faith as described in Hebrews 11:6 will often require you to allow God to supply specific needs rather than depending upon society's accepted solutions.

And without faith it is impossible to please God, because anyone who comes to him must believe that he exists and that he rewards those who earnestly seek him.

How might this actually work in your own life? As an example, after seeking the Lord's direction in a financial crisis, you might decide that indebtedness is not God's will for you. Based on Romans 13:3 ("Let no debt remain outstanding, except the continuing debt to love one another"), you might decide that you will not use credit cards for a particular need, but will wait until God provides you with the necessary cash even though you see no possible source for it now. At the risk of financial loss if you don't act immediately, you nonetheless decide to wait for God to provide cash before you buy. *This act of faith will cause you to trust God to provide money for a specific need rather than using credit card indebtedness that has already been approved by your bank.*

**2. Faith is trusting God (Jesus) for an outcome even when that trust incurs personal risk which could otherwise be avoided.** In this instance, the trust in God remains as stated above. However, this variation emphasizes that the risk is variable depending upon the object of faith. This is, of course, a *perceived* risk because God is certainly more reliable than the circumstances surrounding our lives. Nonetheless, we have accommodated ourselves to society's care for our needs to such an extent that its solutions often are perceived as being more reliable (or at least more predictable) than God's solutions. This definition emphasizes that trusting God will introduce an element of risk that could otherwise be avoided if we sought a normal solution to the problem.

For example, say that you have carefully invested limited funds for your retirement. If you continue to work and invest until you are 65, you anticipate that you will have a small but sufficient retirement income. In your late 50s, however, God begins prompting you to use a third of that retirement fund for a specific ministry. If you use the money for ministry, you see no alternative but to continue working past normal retirement age. You can also see that there will be no extra money available for unforeseen expenditures or emergencies. This act of faith will introduce financial risk during your retirement years that could have been avoided if you had not decided to use the money for this ministry. *This act of faith will cause you to transfer your trust from a retirement investment dedicated to your future income to a personal God who will take responsibility for your retirement well being.*

3. *Faith is trusting God (Jesus) for an outcome which is impossible through human effort irrespective of the willingness to incur risk.* Again, the object of faith is a personal God. In this instance, however, the anticipated outcome of faith is something that is impossible through any human effort in spite of the amount of risk. As in all matters of faith, the outcome must be according to God's will, but in this case there will be no known way to achieve the end result through human organization or resources. Nonetheless, this does not preclude human effort or involvement as part of the final outcome.

Risk is also involved in this instance because God's leading may result in greater potential for failure. The risk varies according to the degree of faith exercised. That is, the task is impossible and the risk is certain. If the task is declined, there will be no risk.

Say, for instance, that God directs you into a prayer ministry for the conversion of a specific group of people. If asked, fellow Christians would agree that the salvation of this group of people would be a "miracle," but they would also generally agree that it could never happen. However, because of the time involvement of this ministry, you will need to terminate your present high-level management job and live on a reduced income coming from part-time work. Your faith will cause you to depend on God to do something that no possible human effort could achieve. Exercising your faith to the fullest extent will require you to make irreversible changes in your professional advancement. *In this case, your willingness to risk future earning and professional advancement does not guarantee that your ministry will be successful. Irrespective of the time you invest, the desired results will occur only if God intervenes.*

### Jonathan on the hill

1 Samuel 14:4-15 tells the story of the victory of Jonathan and his armor-bearer over 20 Philistines:

> Jonathan said to his young armor-bearer, "Come, let's go over to the outpost of those uncircumcised fellows. Perhaps [Yahweh][1] will act in our behalf. Nothing can hinder [Yahweh] from saving, whether by many or by few."

> "Do all that you have in mind," his armor-bearer said. "Go ahead; I am with you heart and soul."

> Jonathan said, "Come, then; we will cross over toward the men and let them see us. If they say to us, 'Wait there until we come to you,' we will stay where we are and not go up to them. But if they say, 'Come up to us,' we will climb up, because that will be our sign that [Yahweh] has given them into our hands."

> So both of them showed themselves to the Philistine outpost. "Look!" said the Philistines, "The Hebrews are crawling out of the

---

[1] William Tyndale first published his English New Testament in 1525. He also translated the Pentateuch and Jonah from the Old Testament. Other early English translators copied many of Tyndale's phrases and translation practices. Tyndale made many excellent contributions to the English Bible. However, he made one contribution to Old Testament English translation that is extremely unfortunate. Though he introduced the name of God as *Iovah* (now written *Jehovah*), he most frequently translated God's name in the Old Testament as LORD, spelled with capital letters. In all but a few English translations since, LORD has continued to be used rather than *Jehovah*, *Yahweh*, or some other suitable representation of the actual name of God. The Hebrew name of God (YHWH when transcribed with English letters) appears approximately 6,900 times in the Old Testament. There is no justification for Bible translators today to use a substitute for God's proper name. Throughout this book, "[Yahweh]" replaces the NIV's "the LORD" in Old Testament passages that contain God's proper name.

holes they were hiding in." The men of the outpost shouted to Jonathan and his armor-bearer, "Come up to us and we'll teach you a lesson."

So Jonathan said to his armor-bearer, "Climb up after me; [Yahweh] has given them into the hand of Israel."

Jonathan climbed up, using his hands and feet, with his armor-bearer right behind him. The Philistines fell before Jonathan, and his armor-bearer followed and killed behind him. In that first attack Jonathan and his armor-bearer killed some twenty men in an area of about half an acre.

Visualize Jonathan's commitment of faith. Not only were he and his armor-bearer outnumbered 20 to 2, but they had to climb up the crag on all fours. You must recognize the risk they were taking. They would be totally unprotected if the Philistines rolled rocks down on them. Probably the only reason the Philistines waited was in anticipation of the sport when the two men reached the top. If Jonathan had changed his mind and turned back, the Philistines would have killed them in an instant.

But God *did* give them the victory. Their faith was rewarded by the garrison's complete rout. The tide was turned, and the entire Philistine army was eventually defeated. Look at verse 15:

Then panic struck the whole army—those in the camp and field, and those in the outposts and raiding parties—and the ground shook. It was a panic sent by God.

This victory was not the result of Jonathan's physical prowess. This was God's work in response to Jonathan's faith. Look again at the definitions of faith. Jonathan was trusting God rather than trusting conventional means of warfare. He was trusting God for victory even when that trust incurred otherwise avoidable personal risk. He could have stayed in camp in comfort and safety and avoided the danger he faced in challenging the Philistines. *He trusted God to do what could not be done through human effort alone irrespective of his willingness to incur the normal risk of military battle.* Nonetheless, Jonathan and his armor-bearer used their best skill and cunning in hand-to-hand combat. They used their swords without passively waiting for God to act.

## Risk and faith; a practical application

In Christian circles, we often hear talk of doing things "by faith." Most frequently, however, this expresses a *risk-free faith* that may be little more than justification for action that has no clear direction or careful planning. On its most rudimentary level, this expression of *faith* may simply be the result of being trapped in circumstances which have unknown outcomes.

Let's use a difficult and emotionally-charged example. Say, for instance, that you attend a church where miracle healing is not generally expected. Then, say that you are diagnosed with a terminal illness in which two medical opinions agree that you have only six months to live unless you undergo a specified medical treatment. Your doctors cannot guarantee that the treatment will be successful—in fact, they warn you that the treatment itself may kill you. On the other hand, if the treatment is successful, there is a possibility that you may have as much as five years' extended life expectancy.

Of course, your church will be praying for you. From that prayer emphasis will come the expressed belief that "In faith, we are trusting God to work on your behalf as He wishes." You and your spouse may also express your faith that God is in control. However, with no further consideration of what God may direct you personally to do, you allow the doctor to schedule treatment.

At this point, neither you nor your church have expressed genuine acting faith. (As we will see in the next chapter, however, there may be true expressions of resting faith.) You are relying on conventional means just as any non-believer would under the same circumstances. Both you and the non-believer live with the same prognosis: 1) death in six months without treatment, 2) possible death as a result of the treatment, or 3) a five-year life expectancy if treatment is successful. For both of you, the outcome is based on medical projections rather than faith in God.

On the other hand, what would you do if you were acting in faith? Your first step would be to ask God to direct you regarding scheduling of any further treatment. You would also determine that you would follow His leading irrespective of what it might be. At this point you would incur risk because God might direct you to trust Him rather than using conventional treatment. God's direction might be quite different than your own inclination. (It is sobering to see believers who are willing to risk death during treatment, but who are not willing to risk a Sovereign God's leading.)

The point of this illustration is not to suggest that God leads those living by faith either toward medical treatment or away from it. It is His prerogative to determine what is best for each believer.

To continue with the illustration, it might even be God's sovereign choice that your act of faith would result in an earlier death than had you elected medical treatment. Living by faith does not always result in the "better" or "financially more prosperous" or "more healthful" way. But it always results in the path that God knows is best for you considering His greater purpose.

———————  •  ———————

*Lord God, I want to learn to trust You. When I reach Heaven, I want to look back and see victories of faith in my life. I am tired of my insipid Christianity. I want to take risks for You. But I am so weak. Help me to trust You, Lord Jesus.*

# 2 What is Resting Faith?

The faith described in Chapter 1 is only the starting point for living by faith. It is marvelous to trust Jesus to *do* things through you that you cannot do yourself. But there is much more to faith than that.

The faith that sets our Christian experience apart from every other human emotion is the reality of Almighty God dwelling in us. His indwelling (abiding) presence is seen in Jesus' allusion to the vine and branches. He does not indwell us for the primary purpose of *doing*. He indwells us for the purpose of *being*.

## The vine and the branches

What a privilege it is to abide in Jesus and to have Jesus abide in us. He is the whole vine; we are branches that are a part of that vine. Not only do we belong to Him, we are truly a *part* of Him. Shortly before Jesus left His followers, He told them:

> [1]I am the true vine, and My Father is the vinedresser. [2]Every branch in Me that does not bear fruit, He takes away; and every branch that bears fruit, He prunes it, that it may bear more fruit. [3]You are already clean because of the word which I have spoken to you. [4]Abide in Me, and I in you. As the branch cannot bear fruit of itself, unless it abides in the vine, so neither can you unless you abide in Me. [5]I am the vine, you are the branches; he who abides in Me, and I in him, he bears much fruit; for apart from Me you can do nothing. [6]If anyone does not abide in Me, he is thrown away as a branch, and dries up; and they gather them, and cast them into the fire, and they are burned. [7]If you abide in Me, and my words abide in you, ask whatever you wish, and it shall be done for you. [8]By this is My Father glorified, that you bear much fruit, and so prove to be My disciples. [9]Just as the Father has loved Me, I have also loved you; abide in My love. [10]If you keep My commandments, you will abide in My love; just as I have kept My Father's commandments, and abide in His love. [11]These things I have spoken to you, that My joy may be in you, and that your joy may be made full. (John 15:1-11 NASB)

Can you begin to understand what it means to be a part of Jesus? The vine is the whole living organism. The branch is a part of the vine. As believers, we are literally a part of Jesus.

From that intimate union comes many promises from this passage alone:

1. We not only have the care and life of Jesus with whom we are intimately joined, but we also have the Father's care for us as branches when He cares for Jesus as the vine. (verse 1)

2. The Father carefully prunes in order that we might bear more fruit. It is not mere hacking on the vine by an hourly employee. It is the loving care of the Master Vinedresser. We are subject to gentle correction resulting in joyful productivity. (verses 1-2)

3. We have already been pronounced "clean." We already share the holiness of the vine. The shame of sin is gone forever. (verse 3)

4. Abiding is mutual. We abide in Jesus. Jesus abides in us. What a wonder and a privilege that is! (verse 4)

5. Abiding is the foundation for bearing much fruit. Sin would convince the human mind that bearing fruit pleasing to a Holy God is drudgery. How far that is from the truth. Producing the fruit of a godly life through His power is the fulfillment of all that Jesus' holiness affords to us. (verses 5, 8)

6. As godly men and women, we have the great privilege of asking *whatever we wish* knowing it will be done for us. (verse 7)

7. We have been entrusted with the responsibility of keeping His commandments. With the performance of that responsibility comes great benefit. Jesus loves us as much as the Father loves Him. (verses 9-10)

8. We have complete joy. Jesus' joy is *in* us, resulting in our joy being *full.* (verse 11)

When we abide in Jesus and Jesus abides in us, it is Jesus who empowers us. It is His strength working through us. It is His love in us with which we in turn love God and others. It is His faith—not our own—which empowers us to act and rest in faith.

Galatians 2:20 says:

I have been crucified with Christ and I no longer live, but Christ lives in me. The life I live in the body, I live by faith in the Son of God, who loved me and gave himself for me.

### Abiding faith

It is an awesome privilege to exercise faith that can be used to accomplish great things. There is a place in God's domain for *doing*. It is thrilling to see God do the impossible through our faith. The faith of *doing* was described in Chapter 1.

However, that is secondary in comparison with the faith that appropriates the indwelling presence of Almighty God Himself.

This faith never exalts self-effort. Nor is the presence of an indwelling God for the purpose of making *us* powerful. God's indwells us so that He can bear fruit through us, and so that He can give us great joy.

The deployment of our lives is God's prerogative. He may produce fruit in some lives by outward demonstrations of His power:

> And what more shall I say? I do not have time to tell about Gideon, Barak, Samson, Jephthath, David, Samuel and the prophets, who through faith conquered kingdoms, administered justice, and gained what was promised; who shut the mouths of lions, quenched the fury of the flames, and escaped the edge of the sword; whose weakness was turned to strength; and who became powerful in battle and routed foreign armies. (Hebrews 11:32-34)

He may produce fruit in others' lives in order to demonstrate His grace through extreme hardship and even death:

> Women received back their dead, raised to life again. Others were tortured and refused to be released, so that they might gain a better resurrection. Some faced jeers and flogging, while still others were chained and put in prison. They were stoned; they were sawed in two; they were put to death by the sword. They went about in sheepskins and goatskins, destitute, persecuted and mistreated—the world was not worthy of them. They wandered in deserts and mountains, and in caves and holes in the ground. (Hebrews 11:35-38)

Having Jesus abiding in you does not guarantee that you will be successful or powerful from a human perspective. In fact, contrary to expressions of how much God will do with a man or woman completely yielded to Him, the abiding presence of Jesus in no way suggests great outbreaks of evangelism or revival. It will assure, however, that your life will be molded and guided by Jesus' abiding presence so that you become everything that He wants you to be.

**What does the abiding presence of Jesus do for our faith?**

Hebrews 4:1-3, 9-11 tells what the abiding presence of Jesus does for our faith:

> Therefore, since the promise of entering his rest still stands, let us be careful that none of you be found to have fallen short of it. For we also have had the gospel preached to us, just as they did; but the message they heard was of no value to them, because those who heard did not combine it with faith. Now we who have believed enter that rest.

> ...there remains, then, a Sabbath-rest for the people of God; for anyone who enters God's rest also rests from his own work, just as God did from his. Let us, therefore, make every effort to enter that rest, so that no one will fall by following their example of disobedience.

Among many other things, Jesus' abiding presence produces the full extent of *rest* described in these verses. One who is resting in God's perfect provision is freed from any anxiety that life may be out of control. *This rest is a perfect confidence in God's ability to care for every eventuality.* Nothing outside of His control can harm us even though we might be going through the deepest trial. The calm is not on the outside; the calm is in our spirit.

This rest does not imply passivity or a lack of appropriate human survival instinct. We will protect ourselves or our family both physically and mentally when it is appropriate. Nor does this rest imply that there is no human response when our well-being is threatened. We may fully understand the potential consequences of a life-threatening disease, a family crisis, or loss of employment. At the same time, we will allow Jesus to control our emotions and responses through His sovereign authority. We will seek His direction in whatever action we would take in medical treatment, remedial intervention between family members, or planning for new employment. But the ultimate responsibility for our well-being will be left with Him. We are fully *resting* in His control and will accept whatever He chooses whether it is to bring about a full resolution of the crisis or to allow devastating disaster.

The reality of this rest is not validated during the pleasant times of life. Anyone can feel secure when everything is going well. Most people can also tolerate slight inconveniences with minimal dysfunction. In contrast, *the context for the rest Jesus gives is pronounced adversity.* It was those individuals who are described at the end of Hebrews 11 who were resting by faith even though they were tortured, mocked and flogged, chained and thrown into prison, stoned or sawed in two, or were destitute, persecuted and mistreated. The physical injuries produced just as much pain as they would for any of us. The mental pressures, the hunger, and the loneliness were just as intense. But their spirits *rested*.

## Resting faith

Let's start with this principle:

*Faith does not negate our understanding of the seriousness of real or potential adversity. It removes anxiety, however, when we acknowledge that the responsibility for the outcome belongs to a sovereign God.* By its very nature, faith would cease to exist if there was no recognition of the real or potential adversity.

Do not think of faith as a removal of your *understanding* or *awareness* of adversity. In fact, if you did not understand the gravity of an impending event, there would be no need for faith. We don't need faith to face difficulties we aren't aware of.

Consequently, in order to trust God, we *must* understand that what we are facing entails either real or potential adversity. In fact, the more potential there is for disaster, the more potential there is for faith. It is that simple.

If faith does not remove our understanding of the real or potential adversity, how do we deal with it? We cope by means of *resting* faith.

In the first chapter, I gave an illustration of a decision to use one-third of your retirement investment for a ministry. If you were financially well off, this would pose no risk. However, if you had just barely enough for your planned retirement, reallocating this amount would most certainly cause hardship. You would understand its future implications. Let's say that you decided to use the money for ministry in spite of the risk. Would God intend for you to begin fretting about your retirement years? No! You see, faith would actually lead you to take a high risk, and an understanding of that risk would make you aware of the fact that you had acted in faith. *Acting* faith would require the risk.

Now you would learn about *resting* faith. You would not fret over your future because you would understand that Jesus made the promise in Matthew 6:25, 31- 33:

"Therefore I tell you, do not worry about your life, what you will eat or drink; or about your body, what you will wear. Is not life more important than food, and the body more important than clothes?

"So do not worry, saying, 'What shall we eat?' or 'What shall we drink? or 'What shall we wear?' For the pagans run after all these things, and your heavenly Father knows that you need them. But seek first his kingdom and his righteousness, and all these things will be given to you as well."

Does that mean that you would forget there is risk involved? Of course not. The knowledge of risk would heighten your trust. However, because of your *resting* faith you would not be paralyzed by any fear of the future.

Nor would plans to supplement your income necessarily negate your resting faith. If the Lord led you to do so, you might pursue a home business that would replace the retirement investment you used for ministry. You would not, however, start a business out of panic or without carefully consulting the Lord first.

I am not suggesting that fear in this sense is even wrong.[1] Fear may be the very thing that validates an act of faith. However, it would be your resting faith in Jesus which would allow you to entrust that fear entirely to Him. *Having given Him that fear, you would become free of its control while still being aware of its reality.*

Releasing a specific area of fear to Jesus is not typically a one-time event. You may be dealing with an issue that has great potential for personal harm. You may often express your fear of the outcome to Jesus. However, as you grow in Him, it is not a process of fretting. It is a realistic appraisal that says, "Jesus, I am afraid. The potential consequences are more than I can handle. Nonetheless, I am trusting You to take care of me, so I ask You to deliver me from this fear." There is nothing wrong with a full recognition of the danger you face. The error is only in trying to quell the fear yourself rather than trusting Jesus to care for you.

In a practical sense, resting faith requires growth just like acting faith does. To return to the previous example, one day you realize how tired you are getting at work now compared with just a few years earlier. However, you realize that you must continue working

---

[1] I am not saying that fear should be an acceptable part of a believer's faith. Our life *should* evidence the joy and confidence of relying on God to provide for us. I am merely trying to emphasize that living by faith does not erase from our mind the potential risk that we may be taking in order to trust Jesus. I am also suggesting that the reminder of the consequences of that risk is also a reminder of the degree of our willingness to continue trusting Jesus.

because your remaining investments are inadequate for your retirement. That thought will drive you again and again to reaffirm your resting faith. You must not berate yourself for reviewing the risk as time goes on. God will be taking you deeper into a resting faith. At age 57 you might have anticipated some of the problems you would encounter, and God would have given you commensurate faith then. At age 64, however, you might have a different perspective of those same problems. Tiredness might now become an everyday reality. God will want you to continue to grow in faith as your perspective changes with time.

Scripture does not make a distinction between *acting faith* and *resting faith*. I have artificially made this division in order to express two aspects of faith. Hopefully, this contrast will help you understand what Scripture identifies as the kind of faith that each believer must practice.

In Chapter 5 (*How Do I Get Faith?*) I will be more explicit in describing steps you can take toward developing a resting faith. However, at the beginning of this chapter I said that Jesus' primary purpose for indwelling us is *being* rather than *doing*. It is His purpose to mold us so that we will be conformed to His image. That is not done by displays of power evident to the outside world. He does that by *being* our indwelling example and by *being* our constant companion. He does that by *being* our strength far beyond that which we could muster on our own.

A number of things may parallel your pursuit of resting faith:

1. Acting faith may continue to grow with increasingly high personal cost.

2. The potential for fear may become more obvious when the risk of acting faith is high; understanding and prayerfully verbalizing the reality of that fear may become a part of your life of faith.

3. Dealing with that potential fear by releasing it to Jesus may become an integral part of your resting faith.

4. Jesus' ability to give you calm and strength will be most evident when trying circumstances exceed your human resources.

5. Jesus may constantly increase adversity so that you will become even more dependent on resting faith.

6. Jesus will never allow you to face anything that is more than He will give you the strength to endure.

7. The joy in your Savior will continually grow as your dependence on Him becomes deeper and more satisfying.

**An update to a previous example**

Chapter 1 closed with an example of faulty faith when the need to determine God's will in a terminal health situation was sidestepped. With a different response, however, the same events could be a wonderful example of resting faith. When appropriate decisions are made according to God's direction, it is exactly those crises that set the stage for displaying resting faith. The circumstances that are entirely outside of human control are the greatest opportunities for placing complete confidence in God's ability to care for every eventuality in life.

———————— • ————————

*Lord God, I want to take full advantage of Your indwelling presence. I want to learn to rest in You. Because I understand that You use adversity to teach resting faith, You can do anything You want in my life in order to cause that to happen. But help me, Lord Jesus, because I am afraid.*

## 3 Is Faith Necessary?

This chapter raises a crucial question. Is living by faith mandatory for *every* believer, or is it an option to be exercised by only a few? If living by faith is optional, we could understand that those who want to pursue the specific virtue of faith would be free to do so, while others could concentrate on different aspects of Christian living as their unique specialization.

However, if faith is mandatory for all believers, then each of us must carefully evaluate that part of our Christian experience.

Before I continue, there are two qualifications that I must make for both this chapter and the remainder of the book. I will often state information in as concise a way as possible. The book would become bulky and confusing if I tried to include every shade of Christian experience. For example, in the heading "Faith and salvation" (see below) two components are identified as the basis of salvation. This does not mean that every individual coming to Christ must verbalize these two steps in order to be saved. The intent is merely to identify the biblical requirements for salvation accurately and concisely.

Christian maturity also brings the ability to look back with greater insight than was possible at the time the growth was taking place. I will often summarize faith from the perspective of this later maturity.

The second qualification deals with the uniqueness of individual believers. God has given each of us distinctive life experiences and unique personalities. As we will see, He wants us all to grow in faith, but that does not discount God's leading in our individual lives. Because I am so forcefully stressing the mandatory nature of faith in this chapter, you must remember this important qualification: *God will not lead all of us to the same **intensity** in our faith or prayer life, and He certainly will not lead us all to exercise our faith in the same way.*

I have purposefully used illustrations depicting costly faith. However, anything you contemplate doing in faith must be carefully and individually considered before the Lord. Never mimic the illustrations in this book as being models of perfect faith.

Learn from this book where possible, but do not be too quick to agree with its content before comparing it with Scripture.

Let's continue with our question, "Is faith mandatory for *every* believer, or is it an option to be exercised by only a few?"

## Faith and salvation

The new life of the believer begins at salvation. That experience and awareness will vary for each individual. There are, however, two components that Scripture teaches must be a part of every believer's transformation from a lost sinner to a redeemed child of God.

1. *Repentance. Repentance means that there has been a radical change of mind.* It does not necessarily imply grieving over sin, a highly emotional experience, or any of the other human responses that are often associated with this word. *It means that an individual must change direction from being a self-sufficient sinner to one who is dependent on Jesus for salvation.* In Acts 2, Peter delivered a powerful sermon authenticating Jesus as Israel's Messiah, verified by His resurrection. There were many in the crowd who had been involved in Jesus' crucifixion. When some of these individuals realized Jesus' identity, they asked Peter and the other apostles, "'Brothers, what shall we do?" And Peter replied, 'Repent and be baptized[1] in the name of Jesus Christ for the forgiveness of your sins.'" (verses 37-38). They needed to change from being ones who had rejected Jesus as their Messiah to becoming ones who would rely on Him as their Savior.

2. *Faith response.* The second element is a response in faith. This is

---

[1] Peter's statement "be baptized" loses much of its significance if we understand it as merely a Christian rite in a comfortable church setting. The Greek word *baptizo* meant "to be dipped." An important secondary sense resulted from the word's use for dipping fabrics into dye. *Baptizo* came to mean "to be identified." In Peter's day, the white fabric was *baptized* as it became "identified" with the color of the dye. Peter was not telling Jesus' former antagonists to merely participate in a religious ritual. He was telling them to "Change direction (repent) from their past response of rejecting Jesus and to become fully identified by His name as Israel's Messiah (Christ)." This was a powerful response to those who had recently rejected Jesus because He claimed to be God (Messiah). (For *baptizo* used of dying fabric, see *Dictionary of New Testament Theology*, Zondervan, Baptism, Volume 1, page 144.)

not a vague "belief in Jesus." Salvation comes by relying on Jesus' righteousness as the sole means of entrance into God's presence and fellowship.   This transfer of Jesus' righteousness to the believer (imputed righteousness) and freedom from the penalty of sin was provided for in His death and resurrection. 2 Corinthians 5:21 says, "God made [Jesus] who had no sin to be sin for us, so that in him we might become the righteousness of God."

Paul described salvation in Romans chapters 2 through 5. He was writing to both Jews and Gentiles who understood the Old Testament Law, and were prone to misapplying the law to a salvation based on human merit.   Throughout this passage Paul is stressing the importance of faith in the complete and sufficient sacrifice of Jesus on our behalf. In Romans 3:21-22 and 27-28, Paul wrote,

> But now apart from the Law the righteousness of God has been manifested...even the righteousness of God through faith in Jesus Christ for all those who believe....Where then is boasting?   It is excluded. By what kind of law? Of works? No, but by a law of faith. For we maintain that a man is justified by faith apart from works of the Law. (NASB)

In Romans 5:1, Paul gives a partial summary when he says,

> Therefore, having been justified by faith, we have peace with God through our Lord Jesus Christ. (NASB)

Thus, we see that faith is mandatory for salvation.   Faith is a required response for *everyone* coming to Christ.

### Faith and growth after salvation

What happens *after* salvation?  Do we grow by faith, or is there an alternative principle that can be applied?  This was the debate Paul addressed in the book of Galatians.   Look at his statement in Galatians 3:1-3 (NASB):

> You foolish Galatians, who has bewitched you, before whose eyes Jesus Christ was publicly portrayed as crucified?  This is the only thing I want to find out from you: Did you receive the Spirit by the works of the Law, or by hearing with faith?  Are you so foolish? Having begun by the Spirit, are you now being perfected by the flesh?

Scripture clearly teaches that we continue our lives as believers by faith.  The maturing process which Paul calls "being perfected" is accomplished by "hearing with faith."

Thus, both conversion and continued growth ("perfection") are dependent on faith. That is, from a biblical perspective, we can say that faith is *always* mandatory for these two elements of the Christian life.

## Pleasing God

Throughout all of Hebrews 11, the writer asserts the preeminence of faith. Hebrew 11:6 boldly states that pleasing God is impossible unless there is faith.

> And without faith it is impossible to please Him, for he who comes to God must believe that He is, and that He is a rewarder of those who seek Him.

This verse states a timeless principle. Living by faith was mandatory in the time of the Old Testament saints. *Living by faith is also mandatory for us today.*

We cannot please God unless we evidence active and growing faith.

## Jesus' displeasure with faulty faith

In Chapter 1 we saw Jesus' pleasure with the centurion's faith in Matthew 8. Matthew 17:14-18 records another time when Jesus reacted with strong *displeasure*. Some time shortly after taking Peter, James and John to the Mount of Transfiguration (Matthew 17:1-8), Jesus rejoined the remaining disciples:

> When they came to the crowd, a man approached Jesus and knelt before him. "Lord, have mercy on my son," he said. "He has seizures and is suffering greatly. He often falls into the fire or into the water. I brought him to your disciples, but they could not heal him."

Jesus then directed a sharp rebuke toward His disciples, though this presumably did not include Peter, James and John:

> "O unbelieving and perverse generation," Jesus replied, "how long shall I stay with you? How long shall I put up with you?"

That must have stung. These were His own disciples—His personally trained men. Jesus called them an "unbelieving and perverse generation." Later, "the disciples came to Jesus in private and asked, 'Why couldn't we drive it out?'" They were still embarrassed. This was not an issue they wanted Jesus to air in front of a listening audience!

[Jesus] replied, "[You could not cast the demon out] because you have so little faith. I tell you the truth, if you have faith as small as a mustard seed, you can say to this mountain, 'Move from here to there' and it will move. Nothing will be impossible for you."

Look at the word picture Jesus was painting. Even small faith the size of a mustard seed could move a mountain. Yet these men did not have enough faith to heal an epileptic. How truly small Jesus was portraying their faith to be. Don't miss Jesus' irony. He was not telling the disciples how to move mountains. He was rebuking them for their extremely inadequate faith.

However, the lesson that we cannot miss is that Jesus is not the least bit pleased by small faith. Is He any more pleased today with those who claim to be His children but find it more prudent to trust insurance policies, doctors and prescription medicine, pension programs, or whatever else they place their trust in rather than Him?

## The problem with idolatry

Why was God so concerned with idolatry in the Old Testament? The book of Hosea has generated much debate. In Hosea 1:2-3 we read:

When [Yahweh] began to speak through Hosea, [Yahweh] said to him, "Go, take to yourself an adulterous wife and children of unfaithfulness, because the land is guilty of the vilest adultery in departing from [Yahweh]." So he married Gomer...and she conceived and bore him a son.

Gomer apparently returned to prostitution. She became so broken that she was sold at the slave market where Hosea bought her to take home again (Hosea 3:1-2).

[Yahweh] said to me, "Go, show your love to your wife again, though she is loved by another and is an adulteress. Love her as [Yahweh] loves the Israelites, though they turn to other gods and love the sacred raisin cakes. So I bought her for fifteen shekels of silver and about [10 bushels] of barley.

Why did God use the example of Hosea's wife Gomer—a former prostitute who forsook her faithful husband and returned to the debauchery of prostitution—as an example of Israel's idolatry? Because Israel was "guilty of the vilest adultery in departing from [Yahweh];" because "turn[ing] to other gods" and participating in the pagan festivals by offering "raisin cakes" was the antithesis of trusting God. Israel placed her faith in idols rather than in her own true God. This act of trusting something else rather than God was an offense that could only be illustrated by a betrayed husband buying his adulterous wife back in the slave market.

### Faith is mandatory, not optional

Scripture as a whole emphasizes the place of faith in the believer's life. The examples we have given certainly indicate that living by faith is mandatory for every believer. Faith is not an option that only a few spiritually gifted believers may exercise. Many other passages of Scripture would reinforce this truth. (As we will see in the next chapter, however, the *gift* of faith is given only to a select few.)

Consequently, learning how to grow in faith is necessary for every believer. There is no excuse for dismissing faith growth. This does not mean that every believer will develop the same intensity of faith. And it certainly does not mean that each believer will follow a similar pattern in living by faith. But it does mean that every believer must take seriously his or her responsibility to trust God in every aspect of life.

Do we have any idea how offensive our lack of faith is to God? When I trust in other things rather than my Savior, am I reducing my attractiveness to Him to that of a prostitute for sale in a slave market? Have the things that I trust rather than Jesus become my idols like the Baals were to Israel? We can understand why Jesus' rebuke was so harsh when His disciples had such meager faith. What would He say about *my* faith?

### The cost of faith

What did it cost so that we might live by faith? Look carefully at Hebrews 12:1-3:

Therefore, since we are surrounded by such a great cloud of witnesses, let us throw off everything that hinders and the sin that so easily entangles, and let us run with perseverance the race marked out for us. Let us fix our eyes on Jesus, the author and perfecter of our faith, who for the joy set before him endured the cross, scorning its shame, and sat down at the right hand of the throne of God. Consider him who endured such opposition from sinful men, so that you will not grow weary and lose heart.

The *cloud of witnesses* were those individuals listed in the Faith

Chapter of Hebrews 11. This includes well-known characters such as Abraham, Isaac, and Moses. It also includes the nameless individuals at the end of the chapter who were tortured and maligned for their faith. In each case, however, the objective of the writer of Hebrews in citing these witnesses was to encourage us to live by faith.

The writer now exhorts to us to lay aside everything that might weaken faith. He particularly entreats us to forsake the sin that will so quickly entangle us and prevent faith growth.

He then makes his strongest appeal, telling us to **"Fix our eyes on Jesus the author and perfecter of our faith."** It is Jesus who is the *author*—the very source—of our faith. It is Jesus who will also *perfect* our faith.

How, then, did Jesus "author" and "perfect" our faith? Our faith was so important to Jesus that He considered the events of His brutal death to be a **"joy set before Him [so that He] endured the cross, scorning its shame, and sat down at the right hand of the throne of God."**

If the opportunity for our faith growth was this costly to Jesus, what should we as believers do now? The writer of Hebrews tells us to **"Consider Him who has endured such hostility by sinners against Himself, so that you may not grow weary and lose heart."** How could we *ever* face Jesus if we allowed ourselves to "grow weary" or "lose heart" in our pursuit of faith?

———————— • ————————

*Lord God, I confess my sin of faithlessness. I have never before realized how much it offends You. Nor have I ever realized how much the provision for my faith cost You. I want to become a believer who truly pleases You with active faith. But in myself, Lord Jesus, I am so weak— You must help me to trust You.*

# 4 How Does Faith Grow?

What should you be able to see taking place in your life if you are growing in faith? Is this growth something that you can monitor? Because God requires faith, are you able to determine if you are meeting His standard in your own life, or must you live year after year merely hoping that you have pleased God?

Chapter 5 will explain how you *get* faith. This chapter is concerned with what growing faith *looks* like. This is important because you can't measure growth if you don't know what you are measuring.

Equally important, you cannot know whether it is faith or something else that you are pursuing if you cannot identify growing faith. There are many qualities mentioned in Scripture that the believer must exhibit such as patience, obedience, love, forgiveness, etc. But to successfully mature in any one of these required areas, you must have an idea of what you want God to accomplish in your life.

Faith has been improperly defined as "Knowing God's will and then doing it." This is a good definition of *obedience*, but it is not a definition of faith. You cannot properly monitor your growth in faith if—for example—you have confused it with obedience.

One last clarification is necessary before you read this chapter. Graphics are used to depict faith. This is simply a visual way of showing how faith grows. These plots have no statistical relevance of any kind.

## A popular misconception

Figure 1 depicts a popular misconception concerning faith growth. The vertical axis is identified as *Strength of faith* because evangelical believers often think in these terms. For example, it may be reported that one person's faith is *weak* whereas someone else's faith is *strong*. The horizontal axis is identified as *time*. Growth of any kind—including faith—takes place over time. Ideally, it could be said that a particular believer's faith has grown over the past year as compared to his or her faith of two years earlier.

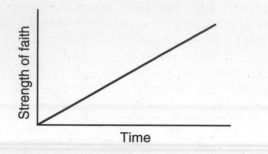

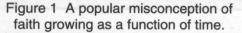

Figure 1  A popular misconception of
faith growing as a function of time.

What is wrong with this graph? It is based on the false notion that faith growth is a natural outcome of the length of time a person has been a believer. Of course, most would agree that the slope angle could vary. A faithful believer's growth might be represented by a steep climb while a weaker believer's growth could be depicted by only a shallow slope. But there is nothing on the graph of Figure 1 to represent what the growth is related to.

*Time is not the basis for faith growth,* even though faith growth takes place over time, as the next figure illustrates. The false notion that faith growth is produced by time is repeated weekly in our churches. The unstated but false assumption is, "Be a faithful Christian and you will, of consequence, grow in faith. The longer you have been an obedient Christian, the stronger your faith will become."

Even when attention is given to discipling, there is often little specific teaching regarding how to grow in faith. When faith growth is not emphasized—or when you do not know how to grow in faith—it will not readily happen merely as a consequence of time. This does not limit God's ability to work in the lives of individuals. Nonetheless, I want to emphasize that understanding what faith is—as well as how to specifically grow in faith—is the best way to achieve a faith which pleases God.

### Growing from faith to faith

Romans 1:17 says, "For in [the Gospel] the righteousness of God is revealed from faith to faith; as it is written, 'But the righteous man shall live by faith.'" (NASB) This verse identifies the way in which a righteous believer grows in faith. It is *from faith to faith.*

In its simplest form, as depicted in Figure 2, a believer will encounter an individual faith lesson that he or she must live through. This will require some degree of trust in God (Jesus) as exhibited by either acting or resting faith. There will be a weighing of personal risk when trusting God versus the seemingly more secure way of depending on conventional means.

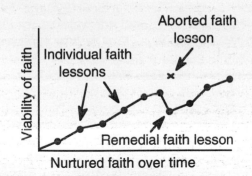

Figure 2  Faith grows as it is nurtured from lesson to lesson.

The believer will then see some resolution to the faith lesson—though not always a complete answer—whereby he or she will see in retrospect how God worked. The result will be a deeper awareness of God's faithfulness and a willingness to trust Him in even more difficult circumstances in the future. Subsequently, a more difficult faith lesson will arise and the process will be repeated. Each faith lesson will be progressively more difficult and will require greater reliance on God. At the same time, each step will be within the limits of the promise of 1 Corinthians 10:13 which says,

> And God is faithful; he will not let you be tempted beyond what you can bear. But when you are tempted, he will also provide a way out so that you can stand up under it.

### Nurtured faith

Notice that the horizontal axis is identified as *Nurtured faith over time* rather than merely *time*. This process of moving from faith to faith by way of individual faith lessons is a progressive nurturing process. In His sovereignty, God, "who works out everything in conformity with the purpose of his will," (Ephesians 1:11) is moving the believer successively through each of these faith lessons with perfectly planned precision and purpose. God's ultimate purpose is, of course, the perfection of the believer in faith.

Throughout the remainder of the book I will identify this as *nurtured faith*. Faith does not "just happen." Nurtured faith is a carefully orchestrated movement through progressively difficult lessons of faith. I am not suggesting rigid "predestination" fatalism. From the believer's perspective, life flows normally from event to event. Yet God's hand is always evident in retrospect; it will be clear that His wisdom was perfect throughout the nurturing process.

I have identified the vertical axis as *Viability of faith* rather than merely *Strength of faith* as shown in Figure 1. In the process of learning to live by faith, your self-confidence will frequently be deeply challenged. The result may well be a more viable faith even though the self-assurance and arrogance that is often labeled as *strength* will be absent.

Notice how the result of an *Aborted faith lesson* was illustrated. What will happen to you if you relinquish your trust in God during a faith lesson? The line will not merely go flat. There will clearly be a loss in your viable faith that will require repentance and remedial faith lessons. I cannot presume how God may choose to work in another's life. However, experience generally indicates that failure to trust God during a faith lesson will have serious repercussions. Repentance and coming back to a place of obedience are necessary in order to regain the joy of growing in faith. Remember Peter's self-assurance in Luke 22:33: "Lord, I am ready to go with you to prison and to death!" Peter's downfall began within hours as he followed at a distance, then denied knowing Jesus, and finally, with increasing intensity, disowned Jesus while cursing and swearing (Mark 14:71). But Peter was not completely restored the instant Jesus looked at him. Neither was he restored after he wept bitterly. It was the women who stood by the cross, not Peter. Even after Jesus' death, it was Joseph of Arimathea who requested permission to place Jesus in his own tomb. Peter was absent. Peter's restoration was still not complete even after the resurrection when Jesus queried him regarding his love. (John 21)

I am not suggesting that forgiveness of sin is incomplete or conditional when a believer repents. But the sin of self-reliance that prevents a believer from trusting Jesus has serious consequences in its disruption of faith growth.

### A more complete picture

In reality, your growth in faith is never as simple as a series of single crises that you can trust God to resolve. Nor do these crises always have the appearance of moving incrementally from simple to difficult. Figure 3 illustrates more of this complexity.

Throughout life there will be a series of short-term faith lessons. Some difficulties will be resolved quickly while others may seem less important in retrospect. There will also be long-term faith lessons. Again, some of these lessons will eventually be resolved in dramatic

ways showing evidence
of God's sovereign
control. On the other
hand, some may never be
resolved and will be
life-long issues. These
faith lessons will also
differ greatly in kind.
Some of them will be
related to your service
for the Lord. Others
will involve mundane
elements of daily living.
All of these
circumstances, however,

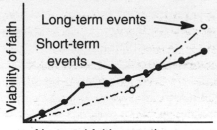

Figure 3 In reality, faith grows as a composite of both short-term and long-term lessons.

are faith lessons God wants you to entrust to Him. It is through these events that your personal faith will become increasingly viable.

## The gift of faith

You need to understand the difference between *nurtured* faith and the *gift* of faith. As you saw in Chapter 2, faith is required of each believer. On the other hand, 1 Corinthians 12:9 lists faith as a spiritual gift which God selectively gives to some, but not to all believers.

Now about spiritual gifts, brothers, I do not want you to be ignorant....There are different kinds of gifts, but the same Spirit. There are different kinds of service, but the same Lord. There are different kinds of working, but the same God works all of them in all men. Now to each one the manifestation of the Spirit is given for the common good. To one there is given through the Spirit the message of wisdom, to another the message of knowledge by means of the same Spirit, to another **faith** by the same Spirit, to another gifts of healing by that one Spirit....All these are the work of one and the same Spirit, and he gives them to each one, just as he determines. (1 Corinthians 12:1, 4-9, and 11)

Figure 4 illustrates the gift of faith. All believers should be progressing in faith growth by way of *nurtured* faith. Nonetheless, there will be occasions when God grants special faith for specific tasks. This is the *gift* of faith. Notice in Figure 4 that the believer who is granted the gift of faith for a particular need is progressing in faith growth by way of nurtured faith. Equally, after the gift of faith is given, the process of nurtured faith continues. Yet God

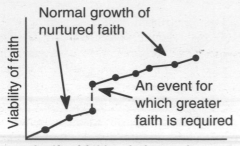

A gift of faith relative to time

Figure 4  God may give a special gift
of faith for a specific task.

intervened in the process of nurtured faith and gave a special measure of faith for a specific task.

We need to avoid an error that is frequently made regarding the gift of faith. Often, when an individual exhibits genuine and abundant faith, he or she is credited with having the gift of faith. That may not necessarily be true. A believer who has spent a lifetime pursuing faith will develop a substantial faith without special gifting. It is interesting to note that George Müller, known for his life of faith in supporting orphanages, education and literature ministries, and foreign missions through prayer alone, insisted that he did not have the gift of faith.[1] He claimed that his faith was merely what God expects of all believers. He started learning to live by faith in his mid twenties when he asked the two congregations he was pastoring to cancel his salary. Then on the basis of Matthew 6, he and his wife took the needs of their daily living to God in prayer, determining never to mention their need to others. God supplied and George and Mary Müller's faith grew.

May I suggest that there is a reason why we like to attribute gifting to those who have substantial faith? How would you feel talking to George Müller if he told you that he did not have the gift of faith; that his faith was only what God expects of all believers? It would be terribly intimidating!

---

[1] "Müller denied that the faith which enabled him to found his Orphan Homes was a special gift. He wrote: 'It is not true that my faith is that gift of faith which is spoken of in I Corinthians 1:9....It is the selfsame faith which is found in *every believer,* and the growth of which I am most sensible of to myself; for, by little and little, it has been increasing for the last forty-three years....Oh! I beseech you, do not think me an extra-ordinary believer, having privileges above other of God's dear children, which they cannot have; nor look on my way of acting as something that would not do for other believers.'" (*George Müller Delighted in God,* Roger Steer, page 310.)

**Faith and discerning God's will**

Let's look at a final graph in Figure 5. The question will eventually be raised, "If we grow in faith, won't we find it increasingly easy to discern God's will when we need His direction?"

Interestingly, this is generally not the case, though I must be careful not to presume how God must act. As you grow in faith, you will realize why it was easy to discern God's will earlier and more difficult later. In the early days of your growth in faith, you had a less viable faith. Consequently, you had less ability to wait on God and you felt more dependent on immediate confirmation of His will concerning some particular action. Then, as your faith grew, He wanted you to rely less on a sense of *direction*, and more on Him as a Person.

Do you see what was happening in those early days of faith when you had a clear sense of God's direction? Look back on that period of time and you will realize that your confidence was based on the circumstances of the direction. You could have said something like, "I know it was God's will because I had this deep conviction that He was leading me to do it. Then in the weeks that

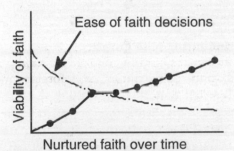

Ease of faith decisions

Viability of faith

Nurtured faith over time

Figure 5 As the believer grows in faith, discerning God's will often becomes more difficult.

followed, several events unequivocally confirmed that the decision was correct." I do not want to demean those early encounters with God's leading. They were genuine and moving experiences, and they required an exercise of faith commensurate with your level of faith at the time. Nonetheless, do you see what was happening? You were trusting a "conviction" and "circumstances." Of course, you attributed this to a personal God. But *your trust required that certain experiences act as an interface between your trust in God and God Himself.* As you grow in faith, He wants you to trust Him directly as a Person rather than trusting experiences or side issues such as *conviction* and *circumstances*. In general, there will be fewer of these manifestations as you grow in faith. Increasingly, you will find yourself dealing with God Himself as you seek to discern His will.

To your great surprise, there will be no answer at times when you are actively pursuing God's direction for something that you feel is entirely His will. You will feel that you must have His direction so that you are doing exactly what He wants. You will not want to proceed on your own because you want His full blessing and timing. And you will be certain that your life is right before the Lord.

Yet, Heaven will be silent. The answer isn't "Yes." The answer isn't "No." There isn't even "Wait." *There simply will be no answer.*

This is probably not what you expected. As faith grows, you anticipated that it would become easier to discern God's will. There is truth to that. The more intimately you know Him and trust Him, the more He will lead you. This does not mean, however, that God will begin giving you clear direction for each decision of your life.

Remember, you are growing in *faith*. This will often require you to trust God more as a Person when there is no tangible answer.

## Monitoring faith growth

This chapter began by suggesting that you need to be able to monitor your faith growth. That should be less complicated now that you realize that faith growth is your response to *individual faith lessons*. You are acting in faith during a specific faith lesson if you trust God to handle that event. You are not acting in faith if you rely solely on yourself or on conventional means without seeking God's direction.[2]

In a similar way, you can evaluate how you handle faith lessons today in comparison with how you handled them a year ago. That will indicate to you how you have grown in faith over the past year.

Abraham grew in faith. We can determine that by monitoring his responses to individual faith lessons.

When God first called Abram in Genesis 12:1-2, He told Abram to "Leave your country, your people and your father's household and go to the land I will show you. I will make you into a great nation and I will

---

2 Conventional means and faith are not mutually exclusive. Conventional means may often be a part of God's provision. However, faith requires that God will be your primary recourse during adversity. You will turn initially to God rather than trusting *solely* or *initially* in conventional means. From the outside, others may be unable to evaluate your motives when you face adversity, but privately you will know when you are placing your trust primarily in God even though you may use conventional means. (Review the discussion in Chapter 1 under the first definition of faith.)

bless you." Nonetheless, even though Abram left Haran, he still relied on selected conventional means of his day. For example, against God's direction to "leave your people," he took his nephew Lot with him so that his entourage would include extended family.

You see this same pattern throughout Abraham's life. He faced faith lessons that became progressively more difficult. Sometimes he did well and at other times he faltered. In Genesis 12, he went to Egypt and let his wife Sarai (later Sarah) be taken into Pharaoh's house; this was a poor and cowardly response which indicated that he was not trusting God. In Genesis 13, he finally separated from Lot when he allowed Lot to choose the best land; this was a good response that counterbalanced his poor initial response. In Genesis 15, God reaffirmed His promise that Abram would have a child. Abram's response was initially good when he entered into a covenant with God, but then in chapter 16, he had a son by his Egyptian slave. This was definitely a poor response, indicating that he was not trusting God.

In Genesis 17, Abram was 99 years old when he was again told by God that he would be given the child he so desperately wanted. God even changed his name to *Abraham* meaning "father of many nations." Abraham was more resolute, evidencing that he was trusting God. Soon after, the promise was at last granted and Isaac was born. Finally, in Genesis 22:2 after many faith lessons, God spoke to Abraham saying, "'Take your son, your only son, Isaac, whom you love, and go to the region of Moriah. Sacrifice him there as a burnt offering on one of the mountains I will tell you about.'"

In verse 3, Abraham implicitly obeyed, trusting God in his hardest faith lesson yet. "Early the next morning Abraham got up and saddled his donkey. He took with him...his son Isaac...[and] set out for the place God had told him about."

Then God surprised Abraham. Genesis 22:10-13 says:

> Then he reached out his hand and took the knife to slay his son. But the angel of [Yahweh] called out to him from heaven, "Abraham! Abraham!" "Here I am," he replied. "Do not lay a hand on the boy," he said. "Do not do anything to him. Now I know that you fear God, because you have not withheld from me your son, your only son." Abraham looked up and there in a thicket he saw a ram caught by its horns. He went over and took the ram and sacrificed it as a burnt offering instead of his son.

You can realistically monitor your growth in faith by evaluating your responses to faith lessons that you have encountered. Trusting God with the outcome can be viewed as growth. Relying on your own resources should be considered failure.

Of course, this is an oversimplification. Seldom are faith lessons of such short duration that you will make a single response. Multiple decisions over a period of time are often required  Nor are they so black-or-white that you can either give the entire problem to God or take full responsibility yourself.  In most cases, you will deal with a faith lesson over a period of time and will  make many mid-course decisions.  In some areas of the problem, you must personally act.  In other areas of the problem, you may choose to leave the results with God.   Nonetheless, when you review this faith lesson later, determine whether the general trend of your response was that of seeking God's direction and entrusting Him with the outcome, or whether it was one in which you attempted to retain control.  You are growing in faith if your responses consistently exhibit greater reliance on God.

Similarly, you are growing in your resting faith  when you can see a developing pattern of entrusting insurmountable difficulties to God's sovereign care rather than inappropriately trying to correct them yourself.

### Making mistakes

Will you make mistakes as you encounter faith lessons?  You certainly will.  It is one thing to look back and realize that you did not trust God enough.  You will be particularly bothered, however, when you look back and realize that you trusted God "too much." Trusting God *too much* needs an explanation!

When attempting to grow in faith,  you will be looking for every opportunity to trust God. Sometimes, in your exuberance, you will do foolish things.  Please do not reprimand yourself for those mistakes. God understands the integrity of your heart.  It is not always easy to determine where true faith  ends and where foolish exuberance takes over.

In his autobiography, J. Hudson Taylor related an interesting example of his own over-zealousness.  When he left England for China as a young missionary, Taylor had already practiced living by faith.  Before he boarded the ship for the six-month voyage around Africa's Cape of Good Hope to China, his mother gave him a lifejacket.  (Apparently in the 1850s passengers took their own lifejackets on a ship because it was not the responsibility of the ship's owner to provide them.)  During one severe storm, the ship was in imminent danger of grounding on rocks.  Taylor decided that he would trust God to take him safely to China, so he gave his lifejacket to a young mother. He then spent an hour frantically collecting luggage that would float so that he could get to shore in case the ship was grounded! After the danger had passed, he realized the incongruity. He then spent considerable time in his cabin doing a careful Bible study on faith. He came to the conclusion that God will often use material means to meet a believer's need, and that such means are not a denial of faith when used properly.

Like Abraham or J. Hudson Taylor, you will make mistakes as you attempt to grow in faith. You may fault yourself when you do not trust God enough. But you will be particularly disturbed when you trust God "too much." You will feel let down, foolish, incompetent to discern God's will, or even angry with God for failing you. Don't! Learn from your mistakes and go on. James 1:3-5 is particularly applicable to your need for wisdom in this area.

You know that the testing of your faith develops perseverance. Perseverance must finish its work so that you may be mature and complete, not lacking anything. If any of you lacks wisdom, he should ask God, who gives generously to all without finding fault, and it will be given to him.

———————  •  ———————

*Lord God, I am beginning to understand how much You are in sovereign control of all events in my life. That frightens me. You know that my natural inclination is to avoid the difficulties in life that will cause my faith to grow. But Lord Jesus, I want to trust You in everything. I will trust You to do what is always the best for me, even when it is difficult. I really do want to grow in faith.*

# 5 How Do I Get Faith?

arlier in this book, faith was *defined*. Then it was established that living by faith is mandatory for *all* believers. Finally, various models were given suggesting how faith *grows*. Yet none of this will be truly beneficial to you unless you know how to develop faith in your own life.

## A fact of church life

Almost universally, Christian churches of any persuasion will acknowledge that faith is an important part of the Christian life. This is particularly true of biblically conservative churches.

At the same time, many of these same churches fail to clearly teach *what* faith is. Initially, they fail to define faith in such a way that the listener has a practical idea of how to implement faith in daily living. Worse, there is seldom clear teaching on the process of *acquiring* faith. It is usually assumed that faith will be a by-product of tenure in the religious tradition of choice.

There are four steps involved in developing nurtured faith. The first three are essential, while the last is merely a practical consideration used to keep faith growth active.

## 1. IDENTIFY THE SOURCE OF FAITH

We have already looked at Hebrews 12:2 which says, **"Let us fix our eyes on Jesus, the author and perfecter of our faith."** We can make a simple and direct application from this verse. *Our faith comes from Jesus.* He is the "author" or source of our faith and He is the One who will "perfect" our faith.

Simple as that sounds, we so often fail to see its significance. Who is the source of our faith? Jesus! Who will take the full responsibility for developing our faith? Jesus!

This does not mean that we are passive in the faith-building process. We must be obedient to Jesus' leading or He will not continue to increase our faith.

Yet simple as this principle is—that it is Jesus who gives faith—look at your own experience as a possible contrast. *In all likelihood, you have fallen into the habit of believing that your faith growth depends on your own effort.* You may think that the motivation for faith must come from within yourself and that the incremental increase of your faith comes as a result of your own enterprise. You undoubtedly also believe that you must have some "feeling" of faith before your faith is genuine.

With a self-effort approach to faith growth you will fail.

Before moving on, look briefly at Ephesians 2:8-9:

> For it is by grace you have been saved, through faith—and this not from yourselves, it is the gift of God—not by works, so that no one can boast.

These verses are rightly applied to salvation. Yet there is more in the passage than just the conversion experience. It says that we were "saved through faith." Then we are told that "this" was not from ourselves but was a gift of God. What is "this" referring to? The Greek construction generalizes so that both the *saved* and the *faith* are included in the gift. So God not only granted us the gift of salvation, He also granted us the gift of faith that led to salvation. To be certain that we understand the source of both our *salvation* and our *faith*, Paul added the clear qualifier that "This is not from yourselves."

Faith comes from God. Jesus is the source of our faith, and He is the One who will perfect it in us. *We* do not produce faith by our own self-effort!

## Our absolute inadequacy

We can never be successful in living by faith if we attempt to produce that faith through personal effort of any kind. We are incapable of a self-produced faith. We are incapable of initiating faith. We are incapable of nurturing faith. We are incapable of even desiring faith apart from God producing that desire in us.

Faith simply does not result from our effort. That should be a stern warning to every believer to avoid attempting to generate faith. At the same time, it is wonderfully liberating. Since there is *nothing* we can do to produce faith, then God doesn't expect that effort from us! Furthermore, there is no frustration we must shoulder in not having a *personality type* that tolerates the risks of faith. We are free of any demand placed on us by God to produce our own faith. We need never be concerned because we think we should have more faith, but just can't seem to do it right.

This does not imply that faith is not important, nor that we have no responsibility in pursuing faith. Nor are we to regard faith as a fatalistic or "predestined" empowerment. It is simply never our responsibility to *produce* faith.

Principle #1: Jesus is both the source of our faith and the One who will bring that faith to completion. Faith growth is *never* a product of self-effort.

## 2. ASK FOR FAITH

Paul twice told Timothy to *pursue* faith.

But you, man of God, flee from all this, and pursue righteousness, godliness, faith, love, endurance and gentleness. (1 Timothy 6:11)

Again, Paul told Timothy:

Flee the evil desires of youth, and pursue righteousness, faith, love and peace, along with those who call on the Lord out of a pure heart. (2 Timothy 2:22)

The first thing we notice in the injunction to "pursue faith" is the implication that faith does not automatically grow over time. There is something which Timothy—and by application, we—must actively do in order to grow in faith. We must pursue faith or it will not grow.

The Greek word *dioko* used for *pursue* is interesting. It is used some 30 times in the New Testament to mean *to persecute* or *to be persecuted*. This immediately suggests Saul of Tarsus on his way to Damascus, zealously *pursuing* Christians. In Acts 22 Paul described his life in Judaism to the angry mob in Jerusalem:

"I persecuted (*dioko* ) the followers of this Way to their death, arresting both men and women and throwing them into prison." (Acts 22:4)

Then Paul recounted his encounter with Jesus:

"About noon as I came near Damascus, suddenly a bright light from heaven flashed around me. I fell to the ground and heard a voice say to me, 'Saul! Saul! why do you persecute (*dioko* ) me?' "'Who are you, Lord?' I asked. "'I am Jesus of Nazareth, whom you are persecuting (*dioko* ),' he replied." (Acts 22:6-8)

Paul used this same word when he told Timothy to *pursue* faith, "But you, man of God...pursue (*dioko* )...faith." (1 Timothy 6:11. See also 2 Timothy 2:22.)

We cannot miss the intensity of the word *pursue*. Paul was not suggesting a casual search for faith. He was telling Timothy to go after faith with abandon and total commitment.

Certainly, pursuing faith is all-inclusive of every activity leading to faith growth. At the center of those things leading to faith growth, however, will be waiting on God for faith. In other words, *we must ask for faith in prayer.*

How often do you ask God for faith? How much time do you spend *intently* asking for faith? In part, that is certainly some of the reason we see such little faith growth. As believers we seldom ask for faith. James 4: 2 says, "You do not have, because you do not ask God." The positive side is Jesus' promise:

"Ask and it will be given to you; seek and you will find; knock and the door will be opened to you, for everyone who asks receives; he who seeks finds; and to him who knocks, the door will be opened." (Matthew 7:7-8)

If that is not enough, Jesus then promised,

"I tell you the truth, if you have faith and do not doubt, not only can you do what was done to the fig tree [which withered after Jesus cursed it], but also you can say to this mountain, 'Go, throw yourself into the sea,' and it will be done. *If you believe, you will receive whatever you ask for in prayer.*" (Matthew 21:21-22. Emphasis added.)

There is an assumed qualification in the promise, "If you believe, you will receive whatever you ask for in prayer." We cannot pray contrary to God's will and receive our request. So we must ask, "Is it God's will that I have faith?" Granted, God may lead us in faith growth differently than we anticipated. But it is *always* God's will that we have faith. It is "impossible to please God" without faith. Consequently, we can re-state the promise saying, "If you believe, you will receive faith when you ask for it in prayer."

You do not need to artificially create a dilemma claiming that if you do not have faith to believe, you cannot ask for faith. Earlier we looked at the account of the healing of the epileptic boy in Matthew's Gospel. However, the parallel account in Mark 9 adds an interesting interchange between Jesus and the father:

Jesus asked the boy's father, "How long has he been like this?" "From childhood," he answered. "It has often thrown him into fire or water to kill him. But if you can do anything, take pity on us and help us." "'If you can'?" said Jesus. "Everything is possible for him who believes." (Mark 9:21-23)

Jesus confronted the father with his own wavering faith. The father's statement to Jesus shows that he was desperate for the well-being of his son as well as his own need for faith. The father's cry to Jesus was one that He must find great pleasure in hearing from all of us:

> Immediately the boy's father exclaimed, "I do believe; help me overcome my unbelief!" (Mark 9:24)

Jesus then generously responded by healing his son. Did Jesus also grant the father's request that his own unbelief would be overcome? This man's request for his own faith was just as urgent as his request for his son's physical healing, and must have pleased Jesus immensely. Jesus certainly gave this father greater faith.

Prayer will be discussed later. However, prayer is a vital part of the process leading to faith growth. Ask God intently and incessantly for faith. Spend significant time waiting on God regarding your personal faith growth.

*Ask for faith!*

Principle #2: Pray specifically for faith. Your personal need for faith, your complete dependence on Jesus to produce that faith in you, and your willingness to face the cost of faith growth should occupy the highest level of concern and intensity in your prayer life.

## 3. SEEK FAITH OPPORTUNITIES

Faith cannot grow outside of some context of trusting God. *We are not growing in faith if we are not trusting God for something.* This is where we confuse faith that has the sense of a verb (an action) with that of faith having the sense of a noun (a system of belief). We can be amassing biblical knowledge and mistake that for faith growth. In fact, faith growth that is evidenced by trust in God will always take place in a setting of dependence on God with the accompanying risk of negative consequences if God should not provide.

Therefore, to grow in faith, it is necessary to seek opportunities to trust God. We must *practice* faith. Practicing faith will realistically involve prayer that requests God to lead us into areas of ministry or action that will be beyond our own abilities. In conjunction with prayer, we may then actually plan areas of ministry that will provide for our faith growth.

Nonetheless, practicing faith is not the result of a carefully planned list of activities. Just as we ask God to give us faith and allow Him to accomplish that in His own way, so too, we allow Him to lead us into the circumstances which will produce faith growth. We may undertake a task that we know will require faith growth, but we will not plan activities outside of God's leading in order to artificially create faith.

Nor do we need to seek trouble. We never need to plan our own trials. It is enough to plan a worthwhile objective in our life and trust God in His sovereignty to open and close doors as He pleases. Enough difficulty will come without our masochistically seeking it.

It should go without saying that attempting risky stunts to prove our faith is never in order. Jesus rebuked Satan for suggesting that He leap from the temple in order to attest God's protection of Him. There is never justification for similar imprudence on our part in order to demonstrate faith.

## Practice acting faith

There is no particular order in which either acting faith or resting faith is initiated. However, most of us have probably begun exercising our faith by asking God to *do* something first. It is not at all surprising that Hudson Taylor looked to God to provide his medical school expenses as an early lesson in faith.

You must allow God to lead you into opportunities to exercise faith. Never use anything—such as this book—as a substitute for seeking direction directly from God. Understand, of course, that after presenting the matter directly to Him, He may then direct you through various means. Other believers will certainly be one important source of that direction.

Consequently, you will probably begin exercising faith in multiple areas of your life. This may involve prospective ministry, asking God for direction with personal finances or time, or seeking God's direction concerning health needs or family conflicts, to name a few. You will continuously learn as you grow in faith. This means that, not only will you need to learn how to exercise faith, but *you will also need to learn how to wisely select opportunities for growing in faith.* All who have attempted to consistently live by faith can look back and see early attempts in their lives that were ill-conceived or lacking in good judgment. They have often had unrealistic expectations of what they felt God must do or provide.

There is a risk of making mistakes when you are trying to live by faith. This is most likely to occur when you are seeking opportunities for acting faith. Pray for wisdom and make your best effort to act wisely and prudently. When mistakes happen, do not become discouraged to the point of quitting. Learn from the mistake and incorporate that understanding into your next attempt at practicing faith. Avoid excessive caution in order to sidestep risk. Wisely engaging in personal risk is a part of the faith growth process.

How much should you tell others about your faith objectives? This is a question that only you can answer. On the one hand, a constant recitation of all that you are trusting God to do will soon earn you the reputation of being sanctimonious. On the other hand, there are times when it is appropriate to stand on the mountain top with Elijah and publicly cast your lot with the God who sends fire. Generally, however, it is probably wisest to confine most of your faith objectives to private prayer and careful personal scrutiny. At times, you may feel the freedom to share those objectives with a few trusted fellow believers for their evaluation and counsel. "Going public" with an imposing faith objective should be done only after carefully determining God's leading. If there is any sense that doing so will draw attention to you and your great "spirituality," avoid it.

### Practice resting faith

Resting faith is not something that you must wait to practice. As you are attempting to *do* certain things as an exercise of acting faith, also seek His leading in how you might better trust Him during the uncertain times of your faith attempts. There may also be particular trials in your life that will call for resting faith early in your faith growth experience. These are wonderful opportunities to see God work in your life.

As in any area of faith growth, asking God specifically for resting faith is an important element in His work of producing it in your life. Pray specifically for resting faith.

Nonetheless, a deep resting faith may come later in your Christian maturity. Hudson Taylor had already experienced much in his life of faith when he described himself as "becoming a new man." The result was apparently a great calm and effectiveness that had not been evident in his earlier life. He discovered a resting faith that sustained him for many years in his missionary work in China. (See the book *Hudson Taylor's Spiritual Secret*, by Dr. and Mrs. Howard Taylor, Moody Press, 1989.)

## Cost and the exercise of faith

Why has there been so much emphasis on the cost of faith growth? Though you have probably already sensed the answer, the reason for the cost is really very simple. It is only when you have a great deal at stake personally that your trust in God has meaning.

Imagine that you are planning a particular ministry that will involve a substantial amount of financing. Part of the reason you are continuing with this ministry effort is that God has already supplied almost half of the funds you anticipate needing. Both the initial direction in this ministry and the money you already possess have clearly come from God. Appropriately making the remainder of the financial need a matter of public disclosure is the normally expected way to conduct this type of ministry. Other believers would expect to be informed of the need and would respond as they were able.

However, as you have prayed about this ministry, God is seemingly leading you to use it as an opportunity to grow in faith. You have the strong sense that God wants you to let Him supply the finances without any public appeal or mention of the need to trusted individuals. When asked about your need for money, you feel led to tell even your closest associates that "God is supplying."

The problem you face is simple. You cannot wait to start the ministry until you have all the finances in hand because God is prompting you to begin immediately. On the other hand, if you had to stop in the middle, little would have been accomplished for the ministry. Both the time you had invested and the available finances you had already used would have been wasted.

This is the dilemma you now face. You know that if you simply conduct the ministry in the normally accepted way, you will be able to raise sufficient money to complete it. You are fully aware that raising money is something that you could do in your own strength, though there would be little confirmation of God's direct provision when you had finished the fundraising. On the other hand, if you follow God's prompting and do not mention the financial need to anyone, you face a much greater risk. You will become entirely dependent on God to supply your need as He sees fit. If He does *not* supply, much effort, time, and money will be lost. More than that, your colleagues will feel that you have mismanaged a ministry opportunity.

Do you see why the cost must be high? How could you grow in faith if the outcome had little importance for you personally and incurred no risk? God will increasingly move you toward faith outcomes that have greater personal consequences. That is the nature of learning to trust God—you are not trusting Him for things of little importance. You must increasingly learn to trust Him for things of extreme significance. That is why the *cost* is high.

This illustration focused on money. The *cost* of faith may incidentally involve financial cost. However, the word *cost* as it is used here to describe faith has a much broader meaning. It includes any of those things on which uncertainty or failure will have a momentous impact. This will include our time, our reputation, our professional advancement, our health, and even our family and closest friends in addition to our personal resources and finances.

If you truly pursue faith, you will discover that the cost in all of these areas will increase. In some of these areas, God may choose to let the cost become extremely high. At the same time, your growth in faith will be commensurate with your willingness to allow God to take you through these experiences. You will need to trust Him to provide for both your physical needs and your spiritual and emotional well-being.

**Principle #3: Faith grows through exercise. Both acting faith and resting faith grow from continued practice. With God's leading, we need to seek opportunities to apply faith in increasingly difficult situations.**

## 4. EVALUATE SUCCESSES AND FAILURES (Supplemental)

Faith growth is a dynamic process. You will progressively encounter new opportunities to trust God. There is great merit in evaluating God's faithfulness in the past. Learning to trust God more is precisely what faith growth is about. Thinking back to His past faithfulness in provision or protection will be the renewed basis for trusting Him in present and future faith growth experiences.

However, there is also the matter of evaluating mishaps in our faith growth experiences. It may be as simple as recognizing that you do not perform well in certain types of ministries. God will, from time to time, direct all of us into circumstances in which we are not comfortable. But there is no point in deliberately seeking a mismatch to our natural interests merely to "prove" God.

There will be other areas of mishap in your faith life that will require careful scrutiny. You may discover failures due to your own impatience or emotional or spiritual immaturity. There may be need for confession of sin. Careful planning in order to avoid future recurrence of the same problems may also be beneficial.

In your evaluation you may discover that you were too timid in your faith growth endeavors. Perhaps you held back when God would have led you into more aggressive reliance on Him. Again, evaluate the situation with future correction in mind.

In the end, however, our objective in faith growth is not to develop a *program*. It is to learn to trust God in a personal relationship. Relax. Let God lead you. If you are consistently asking Him for faith growth, you can trust Him to take the initiative in directing your life. After all, *He* is the One who wants you to live by faith. Your responsibility is to allow Him to do what He already wants for you.

Principle #4: There is value in reviewing God's faithfulness in past faith experiences. You can also learn much by evaluating both the past successes and failures in your responses. Above all else, faith is a relationship of trust in a personal God—it must never degenerate into a program of planned activities.

## Summary: How do you get faith?

1. First, you must IDENTIFY THE SOURCE OF FAITH. Faith comes from God. It is impossible for *you* to produce faith.
2. The second step is to ASK FOR FAITH. Pray frequently for faith.
3. The third step is to SEEK FAITH OPPORTUNITIES. Faith does not develop in a vacuum. You will grow in faith by increasingly trusting God. Pray about—and wisely plan for—God's leading into areas in which you must trust Him more.
4. Finally, EVALUATE SUCCESSES AND FAILURES. You will be particularly aware of how God has been faithful in the past, thus encouraging you to increasingly trust Him both now and in the future. You should also evaluate weaknesses and failures in your faith experiences so that you can wisely seek His help in trusting Him more in the future. Do not, however, try to develop programs. Place the emphasis on trusting God (Jesus).

## A closing thought

What would happen if you daily asked God to give you the faith He wished you to have for that day? Would He slap your wrist and irritably say "No!"? Of course not! *Jesus went through all of the anguish of the cross so that He could author and perfect your faith.*

*Why would He ever deny your request for as much faith for that day as He wants you to have?*

Maybe you think He is waiting for you to do your part in producing that faith? Of course not! You can't produce *any* of your own faith. Certainly, your life must evidence obedience to Him and sin issues must be confessed. But He isn't waiting for you to do anything by way of producing your own faith. He alone "authors" your faith.

So what happens when you pray with complete integrity, asking God to give you faith for that day? *He gives you as much faith as He wants you to have.* Perhaps you made that request each day last week. Then in a Bible study class the leader asked the question, "How many of you can honestly say that you have as much faith as God wants you to have?" Would you confidently raise your hand? Why shouldn't you? You have lived that week with every bit of faith God wanted you to have. Of course, next month or next year, you will expect to have more faith. But this week *you are exactly where God wants you to be.*

That is not arrogance or pride in your own accomplishment. It is a consequence of God being free to do in you exactly what He wants because He has heard your request. Claim His answer! Live as though you have faith!

WHAT FREEDOM TO LIVE THE LIFE OF FAITH! I CAN LIVE EACH MOMENT KNOWING THAT I AM EXACTLY WHERE GOD WANTS ME TO BE IN MY FAITH LIFE. I HAVE THE FAITH THAT PLEASES GOD!

*Experience that freedom and enjoyment for yourself. Know that you are pleasing to God. Then live that way.*

———— • ————

**Lord God, give me the faith You want me to have today. Thank You for your provision of faith. Thank You! Thank You!**

# 6 Why Should I Want Faith?

Go ahead and ask the unthinkable question. Why should I even *want* to live by faith? Why doesn't God just settle for a Christian who is living without serious sin, is obedient in loving others, gives generously of time and money, and does their fair share of service to keep Christian organizations active? Wouldn't that really be enough?

What purpose is served by trying to believe in things that can't be seen, waiting for things to happen which are improbable, and doing it all in such an unobtrusive manner that only God knows about it? It sometimes seems as though God makes it more difficult than necessary. He often withholds specific direction or the financial means for doing the job.

These are legitimate questions and complaints from the perspective of today's complacent Christian sitting in a comfortable church pew. Yet, when we understand God's reason behind faith, it makes perfect sense to trust Him.

Before looking at biblical reasons clarifying why faith is desirable, let's first consider some important events that have molded the perspective of Christians living in the 21st century.

## Emperor Constantine's legacy

In the early 4th century, Constantine became Rome's emperor. Because of a dramatic vision and subsequent military victory, he was convinced that God had directed him to rule Rome as a Christian emperor. On the surface, a Roman emperor favorable to Christianity appeared to be a welcome relief from the persecution of the earlier emperors Nero and Domitian. Shortly after Constantine began his rule, however, Christianity developed a very different character from that of its 1st century Apostolic founding. Now, rather than standing united against the common tyrant of Rome and pagan religion, the Church leaders began vying for positions of prominence. Constantine's rule recognized the ownership of church property and buildings. A clergy was established which had political power as well as ecclesiastical authority. Rather than the former threat of persecution for one's faith, there was now political advantage and wealth to be gained by becoming a leading churchman. *The institutional Church took root.*

Not all will agree with my assessment of this period of history. I feel, however, that starting with Constantine, a subtle shift took place in church life that we continue to struggle with today. In the 1st century, the Church was a highly diverse group of people who were united in their acceptance of Jesus as Messiah and Lord. The Church was not an institutional organization with buildings and a hierarchy of paid church staff. Believers were committed to the Jesus they had personally known, and their tie to each other was their common faith and the peril they faced in their hostile world. They had no sense of serving a denominational organization, nor was there a need to maintain church property and programs. *For these early Christians, faith was a way of life that resulted from their life-changing knowledge of Jesus. It was because of Jesus that they suffered, and it was through Jesus that they could hope to survive.*

Today, we can become completely immersed in a church organization that has little to do with a life of faith. The church property must be maintained. The staff must be paid. The Christian Education program must be planned and staffed. There is no threat to life from the local government. Instead, government is just a source of irritation in its demands for permits and paperwork in order to enlarge the parking lot or remove unsightly trees from the church property. *Faith is viewed as commendable—and even desirable—but it is no longer perceived as necessary for survival in today's American Church.*

With this legacy culminating in today's organized institutional Church, it is not surprising that we are asking ourselves if we really need to live by faith. However, *if we would go back to the roots of our Christian experience and rediscover Jesus as the focus of our life, we would find that trusting Him in faith is the bond that gives strength and purpose in a world every bit as hostile to the Gospel as it was before the time of Constantine.*

We need faith today just as much as the believers did in the Book of Acts because the same Deceiver is also *our* greatest enemy.

Be self-controlled and alert. Your enemy the devil prowls around like a roaring lion looking for someone to devour. Resist him, standing firm in the faith, because you know that your brothers throughout the world are undergoing the same kind of sufferings (I Peter 5:8-9).

The Church in North America has become complacent in its presumed safety. As believers, we have been lulled into thinking that we are not in a life-or-death spiritual warfare that demands total commitment in faith to our Lord. We have been deceived. *Our very survival demands that we live by faith. Only a sovereign God can lead and empower us to negotiate the complexities of the evil world in which we live.*

Without faith, we are estranged from the empowering Jesus, allowing Satan to "devour" us in our apathy.

### I want to live by faith because I love Jesus

More than 17 years ago I began the process that has resulted in my current personal life of faith. Nonetheless, I did not start by asking Jesus for faith. Faith was the second step.

My starting point was a desperate cry to Jesus to give me a deep love for Him. *Loving* Jesus is the foundation for *trusting* Him.

In exactly the same way I suggested praying for faith in Chapter 5, I began praying first for a love for Jesus. I often came to Jesus, telling Him that I was His enemy[1] and that I had no capacity within myself to love Him. Yet, I told him that I wanted to deeply love Him. I began spending long periods of time praying about this one issue. Daily I would ask Him to give me as much love for Himself as He wanted me to have. Sometimes, with a touch of humor, I would ask that if it was discretionary on His part, that He would give me the maximum permissible allotment of love for that day!

My acquaintances know me as a seemingly cold, non-people-oriented person who is unable to spontaneously express affection. Despite that personality, God began to give me a love for Jesus that moved me to my very core. Today I am so certain that I love Jesus deeply that it is the most unshakable truth in my life.

Loving Jesus is far from a completed process for me. I continue to implore Him to increase my love. Frequently during the day—while I am wiring an electrical panel or doing other mundane tasks—my

---

[1] My choice of the word "enemy" may trouble you. I understand that I am fully reconciled to God through the righteousness of Christ. Nonetheless, I also understand that even today I have no innate capacity by which I can please God or produce a love for Him. Evangelical Christians often believe that, after coming to Christ, we have a new capacity within ourselves to ward off sin and to live a victorious Christian life. We do not! The presence of Almighty God living in my life assures complete victory. Yet, I still have no innate capacity to live a godly life apart from the power Jesus gives me. My statement to Him that I am His "enemy" was then—and still is today—my acknowledgment that I am utterly dependent on Him for Christian graces.

mind is vibrantly alive with expressions of loving Jesus and my deep gratitude to Him for that gift.

Do I love Jesus as much as He wants me to? Absolutely! He has not withheld any of the love He wants me to have for Him today. For today, it is complete and perfect. He will do the same tomorrow, and next week, and next year!

There is no pride or arrogance regarding my love for Him. This love comes from *Him*, not me. There is nothing in me that could produce it and there is nothing in me that receives credit for it.

Then Jesus gave me a wonderful and unexpected gift. During a memorable time of prayer, He led me to understand that even though my love for Him was from Him alone, He nonetheless relinquished it to me to possess and to cherish as though it was my very own love for Him. *He gave me complete control and joy in its ownership.* It is now *my* love for Him.

Faith is extremely important in our Christian lives. If your life by faith is not what it should be, begin the process of pursuing it with all your heart. Before pursuing faith, however, if you do not already passionately love Jesus, start there. Plead with Jesus to give you a deep love for Him. Pursue loving Him with all of your energy. *Then* you will discover why you want to live by faith.

Because I passionately love Jesus, it is unthinkable that I would not want to trust Him, despite all of my own imperfection. *There will be no greater impetus in your life for wanting to live by faith than the simple fact that you love Jesus.*

> **He who loves me will be loved by my Father, and I too will love him and show myself to him (John 14:21).**

### I want to live by faith because I am a free moral agent

When God created the human race, He gave us the highest level of moral responsibility. He gave us the ability—along with all of its inherent responsibility and consequences—to choose. You and I are free moral agents.[2]

---

[2] Scripture clearly teaches both the absolute sovereignty of God and man's endowment with free moral agency (choice). We err when we attempt to explain one to the exclusion of the other. In our finite wisdom we may not be able to fully reconcile the two, but we must not negate one in order to emphasize the other. Both are Scriptural teaching and must be acknowledged as such.

However, free moral agency is not limited to an initial salvation experience. God also allows me to choose whether or not I wish to live by faith. I may choose to pursue faith aggressively, thus pleasing God. On the other hand, I am also free to sidestep the issue as though I believed faith was for some special class of Christians of which I am not a part. Accordingly, I can choose to sit in my church pew for the rest of my life as an "average" Christian, incurring God's displeasure for my lack of obedience.

Aside from the blessings that will come from living by faith, there will also be a reward in Heaven for obedience in *choosing* to pursue faith. In Heaven, I want to receive Jesus' acknowledgment that I chose to trust Him.

Now do you see why there is such an emphasis on pursuing faith by asking God for something *that we cannot produce in ourselves?* No one individual has a greater capacity for faith than another. In fact, none of us have *any* natural capacity for faith. If some did, then their choice to live by faith would be based on personal ability. However, we all start at the same point; none of us have the ability to trust God. There is no special group that has a greater advantage in the faith life. All of us have equal opportunity to choose to live by faith. *We will be judged or rewarded on the basis of our choice.*

### I want to live by faith so I can trust a Person

Who is God to you? Is He remote—a mere Sunday School God who is distant and outside of your constant awareness? Why *would* you want to live by faith in total dependence on One who has little involvement in your daily life?

Faith is often viewed as an end in itself, as though God wants us to do spiritual calisthenics called "living by faith" so that we will build up a mysterious faith strength.

That is not true. *God wants us to live by faith so that we will increasingly learn to trust Him as a Person.* Faith is not an end in itself. The purpose of faith is to bring us into a deeper dependence on Him.

This understanding opens the door to an intriguing truth. Why does living by faith so often take us through such emotionally and physically difficult times? The answer is simple. Because it is the perils of life that cause the greatest growth and deepest bonding.

We see this every day in secular organizations and events. Alternative youth programs for teens in trouble with the law have often used wilderness camping to modify their anti-social behavior. These camps are rigorous, but often report satisfactory results as teenagers are pushed to their limits. Similarly, the media frequently reports tragedies in which total strangers are united in a common struggle for survival. It is not the easy, normal times that create the deepest sense of positive change. It is the most difficult.

This is also true in our Christian experience. Our faith will grow strongest in difficult times. This is not a faith that is just a "thing" or a "capacity," but a faith that trusts a real Person. In God's loving sovereignty, He wants us to know Him better. The most effective way to learn the depth of His care is often through the greatest adversity.

This is an appropriate place to add a brief comment. As we grow in our Christian life, we do not become *more* familiar with God. Rather, we will have a deepening sense of His holiness and our abject inability to stand in His presence apart from the righteousness of Christ. *Over-familiarity with God is a mark of immaturity; it is not an indication of spiritual growth.*

### I want to live by faith so I can prepare for eternity

There are two Christian assumptions that I feel are wrong. The first is that we live by faith in this life, but that in Heaven we will live by sight. We infer this from 2 Corinthians 5:6–7:

> Therefore we are always confident and know that as long as we are at home in the body we are away from the Lord. We live by faith, not by sight.

Most certainly we live by faith now. We can also be certain that we will someday see our present trials from an eternal perspective of *sight*. Frequently we are given similar insight into our life of faith here when the Lord gives us more complete understanding after a difficult trial is over. Nonetheless, even though we can now see some past events with a limited degree of sight, new events will still be lived by faith.

Hebrews 11:6 tells us that "without faith it is impossible to please God." We already know that this is more than a New Testament principle because the *witnesses* referred to by the writer of Hebrews were Old Testament saints. Therefore, we can safely say that all who have lived since Adam sinned have been required to please God by means of faith. Can we apply this verse to Adam's sinless state before the Fall? The basis of man's first sin was disobedience in the area of faith. Adam did not exercise sufficient faith in God to obey

His directive. Adam wanted to take the initiative himself. Certainly, therefore, the principle of Hebrews 11:6 applies to mankind before man's sin. It was impossible for Adam and Eve to please God without faith.

Does the principle of Hebrews 11:6 apply anywhere else? What issue was involved in the downfall of Satan and the angels who followed him? It was disobedience based on a lack of reliance (faith) on the holiness and supremacy of God. We would probably feel little reluctance in applying this verse to Satan's fall. Satan wanted to become independent of God's control rather than relying by faith on what God knew to be best. God was not pleased when Satan acted outside of faith.

If the above applications of the principle of Hebrews 11:6 are appropriate, we then have a principle which extends far beyond the present age between Pentecost and the promised return of Christ. Why would we think that life in Heaven will not also require faith to please God?

Think of the incongruity of life in Heaven if we did *not* live by faith. It would imply that we had infinite knowledge and were no longer dependent on God. That will never be the case! Consequently, if we are dependent on God in Heaven—and I believe our dependency on His provision will be just as great there as it is here on earth—then we will also need faith in Heaven. Further, we will serve Him for all of eternity. Most certainly we would not contemplate a service that was devoid of faith!

Therefore, it seems entirely reasonable that we will live by faith in Heaven just as we must live by faith here on earth. Now, let's go to the second Christian assumption before we make an application.

This second Christian notion—though it is almost never verbalized—is that when we reach Heaven, God will give all of us a full measure of Christian graces. We feel that somehow—with possibly the exception of some of the great saints like the Apostle Paul—God will endow each of us with an equal allotment of faith, love, and the like. With that new allotment of Christian graces, we presume that we will all start over again in Heaven with an equal capacity to live for God.

At this point, I will not try to use Bible verses to buttress my personal opinion. I will simply state my thinking for your consideration.

I think that believers will carry their *capacity* for faith into eternity with them. (I think this will also be true of the capacity to love God.) Then, if I could speculate even further, I think there will be a multiplying factor applied to the faith I take to Heaven so that it will be increased by that factor's amount. Consequently, if I enter Heaven with great faith, it will be multiplied so that I can operate in Heaven with proportionally greater faith. If I enter Heaven with stunted faith, it will be increased only in due proportion so that I have faith commensurate to the limited tasks I would be capable of doing there.

Let me anticipate an objection. You will say that there will be no tears in Heaven. You are correct. Nonetheless, those with stunted faith will fully understand the reason why they will not have greater faith in Heaven. In fact, they will rejoice in the justice of God and will be satisfied that God dealt appropriately with them without violating His justice by playing favorites. So too, the ones whose faith will be multiplied will never become arrogant. Remember, even in Heaven they will still understand that it is not *their* faith, but is the faith Jesus granted to them.

What I have just said is speculative. Nonetheless, I personally want to be fully prepared when I see Jesus. When I first see Him, I do not plan on embracing Him as though He were a peer. I expect to prostrate myself at His feet when I first see Him as Yahweh Incarnate. At the same time, I do not want to be ashamed of any lack in pursuing faith while I was living here.

Remember, just as my faith is complete today if I have asked Jesus for it, so too in Heaven, if I have been conscientious in pursuing faith here on earth, my faith will be entirely satisfactory to Him. I will experience no regret or shame in His presence for my lack of faith. *If I have regularly pursued faith here, my faith in Heaven will be everything both Jesus and I will want it to be. My faith will please God!*

I want to have faith today because I want to please Jesus. *I also want to have great faith today so that Jesus can give me the most difficult assignments possible in Heaven.*

### Why do I want to live by faith?

We often assume that believers are given faith in order accomplish great tasks for God. Certainly, God uses the faith of some in this way. In John 14:12-14 Jesus told His Disciples,

> I tell you the truth, anyone who has faith in me will do what I have been doing. He will do even greater things than these, because I am going to the Father. And I will do whatever you ask in my name,

so that the Son may bring glory to the Father. You may ask me for anything in my name, and I will do it.

Jesus said, "I will do whatever you ask in my name, so that the Son may bring glory to the Father." A believer's faith that is expressed in a request consistent with God's purpose, allows Jesus to complete a task that glorifies the Father. Literally, Jesus is asking us to bring requests to Him so that He can glorify the Father through their completion.

From the perspective of the individual believer, however, there is a more basic reason for faith than the tasks that can be accomplished. We have already considered the passages in Hebrews 4 that talk about the believer's rest. "Therefore, since the promise of entering his rest still stands, let us be careful that none of you be found to have fallen short of it." (verse 1), and Hebrews 11:6 "And without faith it is impossible to please God, because anyone who comes to him must believe that he exists and that he rewards those who earnestly seek him."

*Learning to trust Jesus is the fundamental reason that the believer should desire faith.* In this simple act of learning to rely more on God and less on oneself, the believer will most completely glorify God, and in turn, will be a channel through whom God can work.

Why do I want to live by faith? So that I can learn to trust Jesus more.

———  • ———

*Lord God, I want to learn to live by faith. I want to learn how to live by faith by watching You—not by accepting the standard of those around me. Jesus, most of all, I want to trust You because I love You.*

# 7 What Should I Do Now?

I trust you are aware of an important theme running through the first six chapters: living by faith is not the result of acquiring a specific body of knowledge. *Living by faith is trusting Jesus.*

Biblical knowledge contributes to living by faith. However, the essence of faith is the daily practice of trusting Jesus with every circumstance of our lives. At times, this will require that we trust Jesus with specific—and sometimes very difficult—tasks.

In this chapter you will see specific applications that will help you live by faith.

## Living by faith is a personal and unique experience

Living by faith will be your *personal* response to God's direction in your life. You cannot pursue faith by mimicking someone else's life. If you want to live by faith, you must learn to communicate directly with the God you want to trust. This does not mean, however, that others cannot encourage you, or even that your response in faith may not be as a part of a larger body of believers.[1]

But you are not alone. Jesus made a costly investment so that He could "author" and "perfect" your faith. He will faithfully lead you through every part of your lifetime journey.

Consider everything that has been said so far in this book as being merely my opinion. I will make just two suggestions:

1. If you are not certain of your love for Jesus, start there. Relentlessly pursue loving Jesus.
2. When you are ready—it may be concurrently or some time later—pursue faith with the same intensity.

---

There is an important truth that should be obvious but is often violated. Once we have received Jesus' free gift of salvation, the

---

1 Faith can certainly be both an individual and a corporate response. By no means is faith the exclusive right of solitary individuals. Faith is very appropriately expressed corporately. Many of the great movements of faith in history were group responses.

driving force in our Christian life *must* be a growing and deep love for Him.    There is no other motivation that can properly cause the believer to desire growth, respond obediently to God's direction, live by faith, and even be willing to face death for the sake of the Gospel.

Do not forget, however, that Jesus strongly emphasized obedience as an evidence of our professed love for Him.  "If you love Me, you will keep My commandments...He who has my commandments, and keeps them, he it is who loves Me" (John 14:15, 21 NASB).

For almost two thousand years, the Gospel has struggled against being reduced to a religious exercise.  If your motivation in living by faith is anything other than love for Jesus, correct that now!

---

The topics in the remainder of this chapter are practical issues you may face as you first pursue faith.   Section 2 will introduce additional issues that you may face later.

### The intensity of faith is unique for each believer

Chapter 3 says that faith is mandatory for every believer.  This does not mean that *the same intensity of faith* is mandatory for all believers.  I simply could not say for myself—much less for anyone else—that I must live by faith like George Müller or Hudson Taylor. Each of us must allow God to determine the intensity of the faith life that He has chosen uniquely for us.

On the other hand, I doubt that many could say that they have prayed about their faith life and then received a firm indication from God as to its final intensity.  If believers will pursue faith earnestly, they will receive a greater measure of faith.  If they pursue faith only moderately, they will have only moderate faith. If they do not pursue faith at all, their faith will be inconsequential. Why not pursue faith intently because faith pleases God, and then let God give it as He chooses?

Under no circumstances, however, are we competing with others. If I am pursuing faith intently, then God is producing in me the life of faith He expects of me.  I have no need to compare my life with anyone else's whether it be the Apostle Paul's or that of some member of my own church.

When I started praying for faith some fifteen years ago, I had no idea how that request would be answered.  As I now look back from today's vantage point, I am amazed at what God has done.  It is beyond anything I could have imagined then. Equally, from this vantage point I can only speculate what God might still do in the future. I don't need to know now what that will be.

## The intensity of faith will vary in your own life

I don't know how God will lead you as you live by faith. My own observation, however, is that God has been selective in the areas of my life in which He wants me to trust Him. Let me use a personal illustration because it demonstrates this selectivity. In many instances, God has led me to trust Him rather than too readily using medication or medical assistance from doctors. I often avoid using even aspirin so that I will not become dependent on over-the-counter medication because I want to place my full trust in Him. On the other hand, I am a diabetic and have been insulin-dependent for over thirty years. I would die without it. Why not discard the insulin and trust Him with that also? I have sometimes wondered about that apparent inconsistency. To the best of my imperfect ability to discern God's will, the answer is simply that God has apparently led me to apply the criteria of faith in some areas of medicine, without applying it equally in every situation.

You will need to practice discernment as you begin to live by faith. There are countless areas in your life in which you could trust God alone without using conventional means. God may direct you to trust Him in one or two of those areas. Trust Him with those things He wants you to change, but do not overreact by trying to make everything logically consistent. He may want you to trust Him in one specific financial area in a certain way without asking you to make a similar change in all financial areas.

These are not changes required because of the violation of biblical principles or because there is known sin. These are discretionary areas of change that have the purpose of enhancing your life of faith.

The day may come when something God directed you to do in a certain way in the past will now seem to be inconsequential. To the best of your ability to discern, it will seem as though His leading in that issue has changed. At one time you were led to urgently pray for something (or someone) only to struggle with a sense of failure now when you realize that your interest in that area has waned. Let God lead you both *into* and *out of* focus areas as you live by faith.

**Trusting Jesus**

I do not think primarily in terms of *faith*. Rather, I think in terms of *trusting Jesus*. To me, the terms *faith* and *trusting Jesus* (or *trusting God*) are interchangeable. Nevertheless, it seems less hypothetical when I say, "Jesus, I want to *trust* you completely" rather than praying, "Jesus, I want to have complete *faith* in You."

In a similar way, I have personalized my faith as being a trust I place in *Jesus*. I certainly understand my dependence on God (meaning the Godhead—I address the Father as *Father*). Yet, having searched the issue in Scripture, I believe that because Jesus became a man, I can relate to Him as the tangible representative of the Godhead. Therefore, my most intimate prayer is addressed to Jesus. I address any of the three by name—Father, Jesus, or Spirit—but I most frequently use the name *Jesus*. I address them *corporately* as *God* or *Yahweh*. (I also delight in using two other titles of Jesus to remind me of who He is; *Sovereign Lord God* and *Creator God*. When I am addressing Jesus with these titles, I am acknowledging His grandeur or His power respectively. If *Creator God* as a title for Jesus raises questions, read Colossians 1:12–23.)

**Faith is an exercise of your own choice**

Living by faith is *not* a matter of following prescribed religious dictates. Increasingly, your life will become more *internally* directed rather than being directed by outside influences. Though you will become increasingly interested in ministry involvement, this does not mean that you should take on more church activities. You will increasingly find that ministry opportunities will result from your personal prayer time, even though these ministries may take place in your church or other Christian organizations. In all likelihood, your ministry emphasis will move you away from preserving religious institutions and toward ministries to people.

You will discover that the decision to aggressively pursue living by faith must be your own. You must become less dependent on others in structuring your Christian life. Because of the high cost you will encounter in living by faith, you must ultimately make this decision for yourself.

Neither coercion nor programming will produce faith in others. The biblical pattern for reproducing faith is by *modeling* faith. Paul modeled his faith for many believers such as Timothy, Titus, Luke, Priscilla, Euodia and Syntyche. Many of these individuals themselves became men and women of faith in their own right.

## Solitude

Allow for my subjectivity in this section describing solitude. If you are intent on pursuing faith it will require that you spend considerable time with Jesus in prayer, and that you learn to discern His unique and personal leading. This will require some degree of solitude. My own pursuit of faith began when I converted a small utility room at the back of our garage into a study. It was there that I first had sufficient privacy to pray and think without distraction. I know another layman who laid down several sheets of plywood on the joists in his attic. During the years his children were growing up, his attic was his private place where he could be alone with God in study and prayer.

Unless you live alone, you will most certainly need to establish a time and place where you can spend undisturbed time in prayer.

Evangelical churches today often extol the gregarious personality as being the ideal for the Christian life. The person who delights in radiant-smile-back-patting-touching-hugging-and-small-group-participation is identified as the ideal Christian. The truth is, no personality type is any more suited to Christian growth than another. Each individual—irrespective of their personality type—have both strengths and weaknesses in developing Christian maturity. Certainly, the gregarious person works well in building social institutions. But a life lived by faith is *not* a social institution. It is a life of trusting Jesus.

Those of us who enjoy solitude must be careful that we do not abuse this inclination. Nonetheless, the positive side of our personality type may be the ability to avoid unhealthy dependence on others' encouragement and opinions. (I am talking about a healthy personality that enjoys solitude, not a dysfunctional personality.) Living by faith will often be a lonely venture. Increasingly, you will need to be self-motivated rather than relying on outside encouragement to continue pursuing faith. Solitude will help prepare you to pursue faith when others around you give faith low priority.

If you enjoy solitude, feel the freedom to develop that as a strength in your life with the Lord. If you have neglected to develop times of solitude, you may need to begin developing that habit now if you want to live by faith.

## We all begin faith at the same starting point

There is a notion that seminary or Bible school training produces faith. It does not. *Nurtured faith* can only grow through trusting Jesus. The theologian and the layman have the same starting point for faith. Academic study does not produce faith.

Before I entered the trades, I had finished seminary and spent 17 years in full-time ministry. But it was not the seminary education that prepared me to live by faith. The most memorable early event in my life of faith took place when I was 21. My doctor said, "You have diabetes." The following week I began to grapple with the real life meaning of the sovereignty of God.

It was almost 20 years later while I was working as an apprentice electrician, however, that I began asking Jesus to produce faith in me. Because I didn't understand the process, I was unaware at that time of the effect that request would have on my life.

*Every believer,* with—or without—a formal Bible education, *must start at the same place when pursuing faith. You have neither advantage nor disadvantage when compared with any other believer.* You must begin your life of faith by asking Jesus for it, and then trusting Him for its growth.

## Godly living

Early in your experience of pursuing faith, you must deal decisively with godliness. This is such an important topic that Chapter 10 is devoted exclusively to it.

You must realize that you cannot live by faith while you are simultaneously compromising God's standards of holiness in your life.

There is great laxity in evangelical churches regarding holiness in Christian living. If you pursue faith, you may feel that you are alone in desiring holiness.

You will need to look carefully at Chapter 10. *Be aware that godly living is a mandatory part of the decision to pursue faith.*

## How long will it take?

You will want to know how long it will take before you experience substantial growth in faith. I can't give you an answer. *Foxe's Book of Martyrs* and similar accounts of the persecuted Church tell of believers who were martyred after they had known Jesus for only a few months. Their faith grew quickly! For most of us, however, God may choose to work at a slower rate. Let Jesus determine the rate at which He wants you to learn to live by faith. You are only responsible for pursuing faith with an obedient heart—Jesus will plan the lessons and the time schedule.

Remember this: if you ask Jesus for the faith He wants to give you for that day—and if you are certain that your life is free from known sin which would hinder that faith—you can be assured that you will be given as much faith as He wants you to have.[2]

However, I would expect your experience to be similar to my own. You may see little change in your day-to-day life. One day God will open a door to a new area of faith and you will realize that your faith has grown considerably. You will realize that you could not have handled the same situation in faith six months or a year earlier. You may be surprised at how much your trust in Jesus has grown.

## Living by faith is always uncertain

Our natural inclination is to want to become so skilled in living by faith that it becomes predictable and comfortable. However, that is the very antithesis of faith, because the deepest trust in Jesus comes when the known and the familiar are out of reach.

A life of faith will never eliminate uncertainty. This does not mean that a life of faith is filled with constant dread. The purpose of living by faith is to learn to trust Jesus more rather than to develop skills for dealing with the unknown in our own strength.

There is much about trusting Jesus that I don't know. Nonetheless, I expect that the unknown future will always contain the same potential to incite fear in me. It is my reliance on Jesus that is changing. As I repeatedly see His faithful care, I can trust Him more for future uncertainty.

By its very nature, living by faith requires that I will always be uncertain about what lies ahead.

## If your church background is non-charismatic

There is an interesting difference in the way charismatic and non-charismatic Christians expect God to work. Our backgrounds condition us to have certain expectations of God. These expectations can either help or hinder our life of faith. There is merit in learning from both viewpoints.

---

2 This is not a prayer formula which you must recite each day in order to obtain a certain allotment of faith. It is merely a practice of regularly bringing your need for faith to Jesus with the anticipation that He will give it to you.

My own background is in non-charismatic churches. Generally, we are conditioned to expect little of God in terms of His direct intervention in individuals' lives. We don't come to church on Sunday expecting to see a "miracle healing" or a "deliverance." Over time, we become satisfied with our concept of a God who *saves* but does little to manifest His miraculous power in daily living.

I have occasionally attended a biblically-sound charismatic church. These people come to church expecting God to *do* things. They plan extra staffing in the nursery, maintain the building heat, and train prayer ministers so people can stay to pray for an hour or more following the service. I have been amazed to see their *expectation* that God still works today.

Following their example, I began to raise my personal expectations. I began asking God to do more in my life, and I was excited with the anticipation that He would.

If we are non-charismatic believers, we increasingly need to expect God to be involved in our lives and ministries. I am not suggesting that we seek "miracle" experiences. Nonetheless, we need to give Jesus the freedom to *act* and *do things* in our lives. In all probability, if we are pursuing faith, we will realize that Jesus may bring even greater trial and adversity into our lives so that we will trust Him more. We cannot expect God's greater work in our lives to remove us from pain or hardship through miraculous manifestations.

Nonetheless, we need to expect God to do *His* part as described in Hebrews 11:6:

And without faith it is impossible to please God, because anyone who comes to him must believe that he exists *and that he* **rewards** *those who earnestly seek him.* (Emphasis added.)

*We non-charismatic believers need to expect more from God.*

## If your church background is charismatic

If you come from a charismatic church background, your expectations of God may be much higher. On the other hand, you may have unrealistic expectations of how God must act in certain situations.

Remember that a thesis of this book is that faith is trusting the *Person* of God. If you have a charismatic background and want to learn to effectively live by faith, you may need to shift your focus from *what God does*, to *trusting God Himself*.

A non-charismatic Christian who is living by faith may have a better understanding of trusting the Person of God in the absence of miraculous manifestations. That is the objective of our life of faith. *It is God Himself we must learn to trust.* Job was a man of faith. He understood how to sustain faith through the hardest of circumstances when he said, "Though he slay me, yet will I hope in him" (Job 13:15). Job was not experiencing miracles at that point in his life. Yet his faith in the Person of God remained strong despite his continuing trials.

*As a charismatic Christian, you may need to learn to trust God more as a Person without depending on special manifestations.*

## Expectations after faith growth begins

After you have begun to grow in faith, you may experience an unexpected emotion. It may follow a difficult but rewarding time of faith growth. Because of your life of faith, you will long for God's direct provision for you. You may realize that you now *want* His care rather than trying to do things in your own way.

You may become vulnerable in your desire to see God work uniquely in your own life. Through faith, you may have seen Him do unexpected things for ministry and others. You may feel that now it is *your* turn to be the recipient. You have trusted Him to do much more difficult tasks than what you are asking for yourself. Now, however, you feel an emotional urgency to see God do a "miracle" or "healing" for *you*. You may be weary because of some unresolved health need or other burden. Most of all, you feel compelled to validate your faith by seeing God do something for *you* because of *your* love and relationship with Him.

But He may not do it!

Paul faced a similar circumstance. Though Scripture does not tell us what his "thorn in the flesh" was, it could well have been a physical ailment, possibly a prevalent eye disease of the time. Paul wrote to the church at Galatia,

> As you know, it was because of an illness that I first preached the gospel to you. Even though my illness was a trial to you, you did not treat me with contempt or scorn. (Galatians 4:13-14)

There was a common and painful eye condition in the Mediterranean region which could account for the verse following Paul's comments about his illness: "If you could have done so, you would have torn out your eyes and given them to me" (Galatians 4:15). Paul could also have been referring to an eye condition in his closing comment, "See what large letters I use as I write to you with my own hand" (Galatians 6:11).

Whatever the problem was, Paul asked the Lord three times to remove it, but God chose not to answer his request.

> To keep me from becoming conceited because of these surprisingly great revelations, there was given me a thorn in my flesh, a messenger of Satan, to torment me. Three times I pleaded with the Lord to take it away from me. But he said to me, "My grace is sufficient for you, for my power is made perfect in weakness" (2 Corinthians 12:7-9).

At this point in your life of faith, you will need to trust God to give you what He knows is best for you without coveting more.

### Can I revel in growing faith?

Absolutely! Just as in any other area of Christian growth, you should be able to view your increasing faith with satisfaction.

Don't minimize your growing trust in Jesus. When God is truly producing faith—or love for Him, or any other quality in your life—there is merit in recognizing it. Additionally, further growth is best achieved when you are realistic in your evaluation of your present progress.

However, what you say publicly is another issue. Others may perceive your assessment of your faith as arrogance. Many fellow believers will not want to be reminded of their own lack of faith. Consequently, restraint in talking about your life of faith is probably wisest. When it is appropriate, God will give you opportunities to encourage others. Allow Him to open doors for conversation, but avoid antagonizing people with your exploits in faith.

Finally, there is no place for pride. Braggadocio or an attitude of superiority over others is always out of line.

The more you grow in faith, the more you may be frustrated because you want to help others, but you know that it is better to say little. You may experience an increasing sense of isolation.

### The days are still routine

What should you expect to see as you progress in living by faith? There is often the expectation that anyone living by faith will be a radiant Christian (whatever that means!) and have a positive impact for Christ on everyone around them. We often couple this with a notion that the individual will become effective in evangelism.

In reality, if you begin effectively living by faith, your daily life will go on as usual. If you go to work at 6 a.m. now, after you effectively begin living by faith you will still go to work at 6 a.m. If you are employed 40 hours a week now, you will continue to work 40 hours a week after you are effectively living by faith. If you prefer working alone and intensely dislike others' blaring radios in the work-place, after you are effectively living by faith you will still prefer working alone and will continue to dislike others' blaring radios.

Your thought life may require significant change. Your work ethics should improve if you have been lax with company time. Your frustration and impatience with problems and people should lessen. If you have had a foul mouth, your speech should show marked improvement. Time spent watching television would undoubtedly be greatly reduced while time in prayer would significantly increase.

In all probability, there will be changes in your life. However, the changes would not attract attention to you as a person or to your great "spirituality."

If you begin to aggressively live by faith, you would soon realize that your life will continue much as it has before. I recently worked as a temporary electrician in a large food processing plant. A sign by the time clock expressed the sense of futility in the work place: "Here today, here tomorrow!" You will continue to live *in* your world, but will no longer be *controlled* by it,

I do not want to discourage you. God will do wonderful things in your life if you choose to live by faith. But He will not take you *away* from life. Rather, He will complete your life *within* the same setting you have been in the past. God may direct a few individuals into other employment or life situations as a result of their growth in faith. For most, however, life will continue with much the same routine even after they have learned to live by faith.

———————— • ————————

*Lord God, I am willing to make mistakes in order to learn to live by faith. On the other hand, my foolish mistakes may not best serve either Your purpose or mine in helping me to grow in faith. Jesus, please give me wisdom in every decision and action so that I might effectively live by faith as You want me to.*

# SECTION 2

## PRACTICAL ISSUES IN FAITH

This section deals with a number of practical issues and difficulties you will likely encounter as you live by faith. Pursuing faith touches many subjects ranging from an understanding of the Person of God (Jesus), to your own prayer life, to misunderstandings with others that can result when you pursue faith.

# *8* Knowing Jesus

**E**arlier I explained that focusing on a deep love for Jesus preceded my request for faith. However, there was a foundation of biblical truth that came before even that first desire to love Jesus.

All of my Bible background from early childhood through seminary graduation reinforced the common assumption that Jesus is subordinate to the Father. I, like the large majority of my evangelical peers, was comfortable viewing the Father as the ultimate divine authority. It was not until I was in my late 30s that I began to understand the significance of Jesus' identification with Yahweh of the Old Testament.

Let me briefly interrupt my story. In the remaining chapters, I want to introduce you to a number of topics dealing with faith. In most instances, I merely want to call your attention to them for your own study. As a result, I will cite few Scripture verses in the following chapters.

May I restate my earlier caution? Do not copy either my experiences in living by faith or my interpretation of Scripture. You must increasingly seek God's personal direction from Scripture in your life of faith.

Let's return to the story. In a study lasting almost two years, I examined each of the 714 New Testament citations of the Greek word *kurios*. This Greek word is generally translated into English as *Lord*. It was an English study, though I used a concordance that identified words in the Greek New Testament.[1] First, I was interested in the use of the word *Lord* in the New Testament itself. Secondly, I wanted to examine each New Testament passage that used *Lord* when quoting

---

[1] *A Concordance to the Greek Testament*, edited by W.F. Moulton and A.S. Geden. This concordance also gives helpful citations of Old Testament quotations that use the Hebrew name of God. Other references like the *Englishman's Greek Concordance of the New Testament* are also available. The *New American Standard Bible* translation (NASB) is also helpful because it uses capital letters to identify Old Testament quotations in the New Testament.

an Old Testament passage using God's name *Yahweh*. 2

Let me give an example.

In Isaiah 45, the prophet was quoting Yahweh, whom verses 18 and 19 identified as the speaker:

> For this is what [Yahweh] says—he who created the heavens, he is God...he says: "I am [Yahweh] and there is no other...I, [Yahweh], speak the truth; I declare what is right."

Then in Isaiah 45:20-23 Yahweh said,

> Who foretold this long ago?...Was it not I, [Yahweh]? And there is no God apart from me...By myself I have sworn...Before me every knee will bow; by me every tongue will swear."

Paul also quoted these verses in Romans 14:11 and Philippians 2:9-10. Romans 14:11 says:

> "'As surely as I live,' says the Lord, 'every knee will bow before me; every tongue will confess to God.'"

Romans 14:11 is somewhat vague in its identification of the speaker. Verse 9 clearly talks about "Christ...so that he might be the Lord of both the dead and the living." However, verse 10 says, "For we will all stand before God's judgment seat." Consequently, it could be argued that it is *God* "to whom every knee will bow."

---

2 In Chapter 1, I gave a footnote explaining William Tyndale's use of "Iovah" (Jehovah) and "LORD" in his 1530-31 English Old Testament translation of the Pentateuch (Genesis to Deuteronomy) and Jonah. You now need a more complete explanation in order to understand the significance of the name Yahweh. The Old Testament uses four Hebrew characters (which are transliterated—that is, written in English letters—as YHWH) as the proper name of God. In Exodus 3:13 (NASB) Moses said to God, "Behold, I am going to the sons of Israel, and I shall say to them, 'The God of your fathers has sent me to you.' Now they may say to me, 'What is His name?' What shall I say to them?" And God said to Moses, "I AM WHO I AM"; and He said, "Thus you shall say to the sons of Israel, I AM has sent me to you.'" In Exodus 6:3 (NASB) God said to Moses, "I appeared to Abraham, Isaac, and Jacob, as God Almighty, but by my name [I AM], I did not make Myself known to them."

God gave a first person singular form of the verb "to be" as His personal name. God called Himself I AM. The human speaker, however, did not address God as "I AM." Rather, God is called HE IS, or YHWH. With added English vowels, YHWH becomes Yahweh. This personal name of God is used over 6,800 times in the Hebrew Old Testament. The use of God's personal name is abundantly clear in the original language of the Old Testament and should have been carried over into the English Bible in a better form than LORD. However, this is a much more complex issue than this short footnote suggests.

Nonetheless, the subject of the verse in the Greek sentence is the Lord,[3] which is the title used of Jesus throughout the New Testament.

Before we go to the Philippians passage, consider what is taking place. Isaiah made it clear that Yahweh alone can say of Himself, "I am [Yahweh] and there is no other...there is no God apart from me." Then Yahweh made a statement that is uniquely true of Him: "Before me every knee will bow; by me every tongue will swear."

It would be rank blasphemy to say of any created being that every knee will bow and every tongue will swear before him in worship. The context of Isaiah makes it very clear that this worship is due to Yahweh alone.

Philippians 2:9-10 elaborates the same Isaiah passage but clearly attributes to Jesus the worship which is due only to Yahweh.

Therefore God exalted [Christ Jesus] to the highest place and gave him the name that is above every name, that at the name of Jesus every knee should bow, in heaven and on earth and under the earth, and every tongue confess that Jesus Christ is Lord, to the glory of God the Father.

No Jew familiar with the Isaiah passage could read Philippians 2:9-10 and not see the implication of these verses. To the Messianic Jew, they are a powerful identification of Jesus with Yahweh. To the non-Messianic Jew, these verses represent the epitome of blasphemy because they defame the One who said, "I am [Yahweh] and there is no other."

Notice something else in this passage. God gave Jesus a name. What name is that? It is the name that "is above every name." That name could be none other than *Yahweh*. However, the New Testament writers always use *Lord* (*kurios*) rather than *Yahweh* for God's name. (See any of the Old Testament quotations in the New Testament that context would identify as speaking of *Yahweh*. This

---

[3] In every instance in the New Testament where an Old Testament verse using YHWH is quoted, the Greek New Testament uses the Greek word for *Lord* (*kurios*). Consequently, *Lord* is always the correct translation in the New Testament for God's proper name. That is significant to the subject of this chapter. In the Old Testament, Almighty God was known as Yahweh. In the New Testament, both Almighty God and Jesus are identified with the same title. Was this merely a limitation of language or an oversight by the New Testament writers? Or does this blurring of the name of Yahweh and Jesus' title *Lord* carry immense significance? I personally think this is a powerful evidence of Jesus' eternal nature as Almighty God.

would include verses such as Luke 1:46 where Mary would be speaking of *Yahweh* rather than her unborn son, Luke 10:21 where Jesus addressed the Father as *Lord*, etc.) Do you see the significance of the statement, "God...gave him the name that is above every name... and every tongue [will] confess that Jesus Christ is Lord (*kurios*)"?

As I traced verse after verse through the New Testament, I began to see this repeated use of *Lord* (Jesus) in Old Testament quotations which described attributes or prerogatives of Yahweh. The pattern occurs at least 112 times.[4] The identification was unmistakable. Jesus is fully identified with Yahweh. What can be said of Yahweh in the Old Testament can also be said of Jesus in the New Testament.

Jesus is none other than Almighty, Sovereign God.

•

I then began to see passages that identified Jesus as the Creator of the cosmos. Colossians 1:15-18, Hebrews 1:1-2, John 1:1-3, and Revelation 4:11 all identify Jesus as the Creator.[5] Creation was not the independent act of Jesus. All of creation—from its grandeur and beauty to man and the plan of redemption—expresses the Unity of the Godhead. Because of this identification of the Godhead with all of the acts of God, both the Father and the Spirit can be called Creator just as either can be identified as Savior. But it was Jesus who was the active Agent in creation.[6]

The implications of Jesus being Creator are momentous. Jesus is my indwelling Savior. However, Jesus' presence in me is not that of a mere subordinate to the Father. It is the presence of Almighty,

---

[4] The total must allow for some variation in the way each passage is identified.

[5] Do you see the high cost of redemption when it is the very Creator Himself who becomes the sacrifice for His own lost creation? Jesus was not merely an emissary sent to salvage sinful man. *He came because the redemption of those He had made in His own image was His highest priority.*

[6] There is a grammatical argument of *agency* which can be applied to Colossians 1:16 ("all things were created **by** (*dia*) him and for him"). Jesus was certainly the Godhead's Agent. But I object to the explanation that the Father was the Creator while Jesus was His Agent for its accomplishment. The same grammatical construction is used in John 3:17 ("...to save the world **through** (*dia*) him"). This agency does not mean that the Father died on Calvary! Jesus acted as an Agent for the Godhead in Salvation, but it was Jesus who died and rose again, not the Father.

We introduce a great deal of confusion into the biblical account of Creation when we read Genesis 1:1 as referring to the *Father* rather than *God*. (*God* in this instance, I believe, means the *Godhead*.) (See the Appendix.)

Creator God Himself. Not only does Jesus have the *desire* to mold me into His image and do that which is best for me, but He also has the *power* to complete everything He intends to accomplish!

•

Because of our longstanding creedal statements and traditional teaching of the Father's role as Creator, many have difficulty with the New Testament teaching that Jesus is the Creator. Were we to suggest that Jesus is a superior God and the Father is a subordinate, we would be in gross error. Jesus is not greater than the Father, and the Father is not greater than Jesus or the Spirit. It is appropriate to recognize the New Testament's teaching regarding Jesus' work of creation and the various roles of each of the three Persons of the Godhead. But it is entirely inappropriate to suggest that there is any difference of rank.

•

Modern evangelical Christianity has devised a God who cannot logically exist. Some in our evangelical churches today would acquiesce to the statement that the Father existed before Jesus. (This position is untenable if Jesus is God.) At the very least, most are comfortable with a statement that the Father is preeminent, while Jesus—and, finally, the Spirit—have some hierarchical rank lower than the Father. Most see the Father as the One in ultimate control, giving direction to Jesus and the Spirit.

This notion is pure gnosticism, the heresy that engrafted itself into Christianity in the latter part of the 1st century and has never entirely disappeared since. In its simplest form, gnosticism was a pervasive philosophy having a Supreme God and a hierarchical order of lesser gods. Since man could not communicate with the Supreme God, the lesser gods provided a means of access through their intercessory roles. Though modern evangelicals do not insert other gods between the Father and Jesus, they generally accept an unstated theology that Jesus, as a lesser God (though they would abhor the term *lesser*), is more accessible to us and can intercede for us before the more powerful Father. They also believe that it was Jesus' subordinate role that allowed the *Father*[7] to send Him to earth to accomplish redemption. (See the Appendix for more information on the Person of God.)

---

[7] A verse such as John 3:16 does not say that the *Father* sent Jesus. It says that *God* sent Jesus. Jesus' incarnation was a corporate decision of the Father, Jesus, and the Spirit, or the *Godhead*.

•

A fundamental truth throughout Scripture is the *Absolute* nature of God. All of His attributes are Absolute; He lacks nothing in any area of His Being. The Absolute nature of God is fundamental to both the Old and New Testament and is the foundation of Judeo/Christian theology.

Therefore, we are left with a logical conclusion. If Jesus is God, then Jesus must be Absolute. Conversely, if Jesus is not Absolute, then Jesus cannot be God. (The same statements would equally apply to the Spirit.) *The attribute of Absolute cannot have rank. Two beings cannot both be Absolute with one having authority over the other.*

Either Jesus is God and is thus *Absolute* in all of His attributes, or He is other than God, in which case He is not Absolute but was created by the Father. Again, the same is also true of the Spirit.

•

If Jesus is Absolute, then the New Testament introduces a dilemma. Jesus repeatedly acknowledges His dependence upon the Father in the Gospels.

The common understanding among many evangelicals regarding Jesus' dependence is that He was eternally subordinate to the Father. This viewpoint sees Jesus as having been under the Father's authority *from eternity past.* The difficulty with this explanation is that if Jesus is *not* Absolute, then He cannot be God.

On the other hand, if Jesus *was* Absolute in eternity past, we must reconcile His statements of dependency on the Father in the Gospels and allusions to it elsewhere in the New Testament. The answer will require a much more comprehensive understanding of the cost of the Incarnation and Salvation. When Jesus laid aside His prerogatives of Deity to become Man, that action carried with it the high price of relinquishing His *Absolute* control as Sovereign God. (He did not, however, relinquish His Absolute *nature* as Sovereign God.) Scripture teaches that Jesus still has a body that evidences the scars of the crucifixion (Revelation 5:6). This indicates that Jesus still acts under costly restraints that He willingly chose for the purpose of redeeming us from sin. There is a profound difference, however, between One who is Absolute choosing to restrict that prerogative in order to achieve a holy purpose, and one who is less than Absolute functioning under the authority of a Superior.

•

This issue is much more complicated than my brief comments

indicate. Any explanation of Jesus' relationship to the Father must reconcile verses such as Romans 15:6, 1 Corinthians 15:24-28, 2 Corinthians 1:3, and many others, yet also accommodate the *Absolute* attribute of God. Regrettably, the subject cannot be developed more without detracting from the intent of this book.

●

In Christian circles of almost any persuasion, there is generally a casual acceptance of Jesus' coming to earth.

If I asked you to list details needing to be resolved if it had been the *Father* who had come to earth, you would quickly see the difficulty of the task. Assuming that you held a traditional viewpoint of the Father as the Superior God, you would see the complexity of the arrangements necessary if Almighty God were to be absent from a position of control for 33 years.

You would also see the immense gap between the holiness of the Almighty and the sinfulness of the people He was living among. You would struggle with the mere *possibility* that the God of the Bible could live a human existence on earth.

You would see numerous difficulties ranging from the human birth of the most Sovereign God, to the death of the Almighty on a Roman cross, to His weariness during ministry even though He was all-powerful. You would be hard-pressed to explain how the entire cosmos could be sustained in the absence of the Father.

If you could look ahead, you would also realize the ramifications of the Father assuming a body throughout the remainder of eternity with all the inherent limitations of that physical existence. Had the Father been the Incarnate Savior, the cost of Salvation would seem staggering.

Why was it any different when Jesus came?

●

It is one thing to recite attributes of Jesus in a doctrinal statement or creed. It is quite another to view this Jesus Who indwells me as the Absolute Sovereign, Creator, and Redeemer. As I began to understand the grandeur and holiness of my Savior, I began to realize what He was capable of doing in my life.

Knowing Jesus better gave me a deep desire to love and trust Him.

●

There are many false dogmas in gnosticism besides that of multiple gods of descending power. A second is that there is secret knowledge that is obtainable by only an elite class.

There is no esoteric knowledge of Jesus that is restricted to a certain class of Christians. There is no deep love for Jesus that is available to only a few. There is no life of faith that is attainable by a limited elect.

*Any* believer can purpose to know Jesus. *Any* believer can pursue loving Jesus and living by faith.

Sadly, however, not all do!

•

At some point in my growing love for Jesus, I questioned the propriety of emphasizing a love for Jesus rather than a love for God. John 14:21 says,

He who loves Me shall be loved by My Father, and I will love him, and will disclose Myself to him. (NASB)

This verse seemed to answer several of my questions. First, it is apparent that the Father welcomes our love for Jesus because it is precisely for this reason that the Father will in turn love us. The Father delights in our devotion to Jesus.

However, there are two other benefits that result from loving Jesus. Jesus tells us that if we love Him deeply, He will return our love in a way that will become a great delight.

There is another benefit that is astounding. If we love Jesus, He will *disclose* Himself to us. Certainly, we could expect that we would learn more about Jesus through careful Bible study. However, that is not what this verse says. Jesus said that *if we love Him, He will disclose more of who He is to us!*

As stated earlier, I also think it is appropriate to focus our love on Jesus because of the Incarnation. There is an understandable link to *this* Person of the Godhead because He shared our humanity.

As a practical matter, however, I often pray about loving the Father and the Spirit in the same way I pray about loving Jesus. I also make it a point to express my love for God. (By this I mean the corporate Godhead. I often address Him as *Yahweh.*)

It would be entirely inappropriate to focus attention exclusively on Jesus.

•

Pursuing a deep love for Jesus or a life of faith does not spring from an innate need. Rather, as we learn who Jesus is in all of His grandeur and holiness, we are then compelled to love Him and trust Him by faith because of who He is.

God will work in your life in the way He has chosen uniquely for you. Experience suggests, however, that *a reverential knowledge of Jesus will be a precursor to an active life of faith.* How could you trust someone that you hardly knew? Why would you want to live by faith with its intended purpose of learning to know Jesus better if you were not intent on knowing Him in the first place?

This Jesus is Sovereign, Almighty God!

•

In order to live by faith, we must understand the God we are trusting. An active faith life is not contingent on understanding a prescribed body of theological information. Nonetheless, understanding the interrelationship of the Father, Jesus, and the Spirit will have a bearing on the effectiveness of our life of faith. For this reason, an Appendix entitled *The Person of God* has been added to this book.

———— • ————

# 9 The Sovereignty of God

The Old Testament writers always portrayed Yahweh as a Sovereign God. That which He did was an outworking of His holy nature and will; His action was never forced on Him by another.

When Moses summarized the Law for Israel, he told them,

Acknowledge and take to heart this day that [Yahweh] is God in heaven above and on the earth below. There is no other (Deuteronomy 4:39). To [Yahweh] your God belong the heavens, even the highest heavens, the earth and everything in it. For [Yahweh] your God is God of gods and Lord of lords, the great God, mighty and awesome, who shows no partiality and accepts no bribes (Deuteronomy 10:14, 17).

Hannah's great prayer in 1 Samuel 2:1-10 extols Israel's Sovereign God:

My heart rejoices in [Yahweh]. There is no one holy like [Yahweh]; there is no one besides you; there is no Rock like our God (1-2). [Yahweh] brings death and makes alive; he brings down to the grave and raises up. [Yahweh] sends poverty and wealth; he humbles and he exalts. He raises the poor from the dust and lifts the needy from the ash heap; he seats them with princes and has them inherit a throne of honor. For the foundations of the earth are [Yahweh]'s; upon them he has set the world (6-8).

The Psalms frequently express the sovereignty of God.

Let [the enemies of Israel] know that you, whose name is [Yahweh]—that you alone are the Most High over all the earth (Psalm 83:18). I know that [Yahweh] is great, that our Lord is greater than all gods. [Yahweh] does whatever pleases him, in the heavens and on the earth, in the seas and all their depths (Psalm 135:5-6).

The New Testament also emphasizes the sovereignty of God. Ephesians 1:11 says:

In him we were also chosen, having been predestined according to the plan of him *who works out **everything** in conformity with the purpose of his will.* (Emphasis added.)

•

If God is *Absolute*, then He must be *Sovereign*. His attribute of Sovereignty means that He alone is in control and is subject to no other power. This in no way prevents Him from responding in mercy to those in need. He is not indifferent. As His children, we are often the recipients of His love and generosity as He answers prayer.

But He is always Sovereign. Nothing will ever force God to act contrary to His will.

•

What does it mean to me that God is Sovereign? *It means that nothing can happen to me that is outside of His control.*

I know that is true. Yet it can sometimes be very difficult to trust God as though He is in full control.

Several weeks after I started writing this book, God in His sovereignty decided that I was ready for some additional lessons in faith. While I was sleeping, I had a severe diabetic insulin reaction. I came very close to death and was taken to a hospital emergency unit.

My state's Department of Motor Vehicles requires that any loss of consciousness be reported. With great trepidation, I complied. I discovered that their report form makes no distinction between a seizure whether one is asleep in bed or driving in downtown traffic!

I was notified by the Department of Motor Vehicles office that I had 60 days to complete medical evaluation to maintain my driver's license. Then, because of a communication oversight, I was notified three weeks later that my license was being suspended immediately. My license was reinstated, though I likely face years of supervision by the State licensing department.

This occurred while I was looking for employment. I work as an electrician for a temporary agency because temporary employment gives me greater flexibility for Christian ministry. I had recently finished an 11-month assignment and was in the process of being placed again. Driving is almost mandatory. Since I am in my late 50s, this has been a time of turmoil for me and my wife.

This was not a lesson in faith I was looking for!

•

It is relatively easy to acknowledge that God is working in our lives when everything is going smoothly. But are we willing to recognize His sovereignty when there is great upheaval?

Some kinds of adversity cause us to mistrust God's sovereignty more than others. When something occurs which appears to be *unfair* or *unjust* or singles us out arbitrarily for a hardship which we feel we do not deserve, we are more prone to question God's sovereign control.

God does not exercise His sovereignty on our behalf only in ways that are *just* or *fair*. He is still the same Sovereign God when our world has turned upside down for unexplainable or foolish reasons. This is where we must learn to live by faith.

•

Recognition of God's sovereignty in *all* circumstances of our lives is a wonderful antidote for bitterness. The sin of bitterness can destroy a believer's life of faith. Hebrews 12:15 gives a special warning:

See to it that no one misses the grace of God and that no bitter root grows up to cause trouble and defile many.

•

There is a perturbing question that arises when you acknowledge the sovereignty of God in *all* events of your life. Does this mean that you can never attempt to right a wrong? If someone unjustly mistreats you, must you passively endure its full fury because God's sovereignty dictates it?

There is no single answer to this question. At times, attempting to correct the mistreatment would be entirely appropriate. At other times, however, God may intend for you to face adversity with no apparent relief.

The Apostle Paul experienced two similar crises, but apparently responded quite differently in each situation. While he was in Jerusalem, a crowd of rabble-rousers created a public disturbance in order to implicate him. When Paul was brought into the garrison for scourging, he asked the centurion:

"Is it legal for you to flog a Roman citizen who hasn't even been found guilty?" (Acts 22:25)

As a Roman citizen, Paul was guaranteed trial before he could be legally punished. In this case, he invoked that privilege in order to avoid being flogged.

In another incident at Philippi, however, he and Silas were beaten and imprisoned. In Acts 16:22-23 the magistrates ordered that they be flogged without trial (verse 37). The order was carried out "severely." The next morning, after the fact, Paul refused to be released and invoked both his and Silas' citizenship (verses 35-39).

The magistrates were alarmed because they had acted illegally and could be subject to severe censure from Rome.

Why did Paul seemingly submit to a flogging in one situation, and invoke his citizenship in another? Scripture does not give an answer. I can only surmise that during the incident in Philippi God directed Paul and Silas to accept the injustice despite their legal protection. Clearly, God wanted Paul and Silas in prison because He was going to do a wonderful work in the jailer's life. This Roman jailer would not only influence his entire family, but ultimately—as tradition records—the city of Philippi itself. We do not know if God placed them under this jailer's custody through circumstances that Paul and Silas could not control, or if God actually led them to remain silent, resulting in their flogging.

Paul's experience does not clarify when you must submit to an injustice as an outworking of God's sovereignty, and when you may appropriately act to right a wrong. Paul's two responses merely suggest that you must prayerfully consider each instance before thoughtlessly taking matters into your own hands.

•

If you fully accept the sovereignty of God, must you greet adversity with feigned happiness? I hardly think so. Nonetheless, it is *because* the situation is so difficult for you that you become aware of the importance of the sovereignty of God.

Acknowledging God's sovereignty in trying circumstances will give you an opportunity to monitor your growth in faith. Over time, you should be able to see that your ability to rest in faith has increased as you compare your responses in similar trials.

You need not feel as though you have lost ground if you initially feel defensive. I am not justifying either anger or lack of faith. Nonetheless, a faith which acknowledges the sovereignty of God is a faith which is viable when circumstances are the most difficult or threatening. The intensity of your initial emotional response is an important indication that you can relinquish the most threatening situations to God's sovereignty.

•

There will always be high cost when you live by faith. Great comfort will come when you acknowledge the absolute sovereignty of God. He is *always* in control, no matter how desperate the situation seems to be at the time. An integral part of living by faith will be your reliance on this truth.

•

There is, however, a limit that God has placed on His own sovereignty. In certain areas, He has chosen to limit His work to the will of His created beings.

For example, it is certainly God's will that all would come to repentance: "The Lord...is patient with you, not wanting anyone to perish, but everyone to come to repentance" (2 Peter 3:9). This does not mean, however, that all will be saved. God has also determined that each individual must make his or her own decision regarding the Person of Christ. God created man with free moral agency (choice). It would cease to be free moral agency if God rescinded that privilege on the most important issue of salvation.

Simply because something is God's will does not automatically mean that it will take place.

There are many areas in which we can see God's sovereignty in operation while He still allows mankind a limited range of choice. God created a complete world. He has also given us the privilege of working within creation for both good or bad. Mankind has done much good in domesticating animals. Land yields have been greatly increased for food production. Engineering has done much good with flood control, soil stabilization, and the like. At the same time, God has allowed man to destroy parts of that creation with deforestation, killing of animal species, wanton release of hazardous materials, destruction of land and rivers, and more.

It is also God's will that we live by faith. Nonetheless, He has given us freedom of choice. Our freedom of choice will determine how He directs His sovereignty in the development of our faith.

If you honestly give God permission to do *anything* in your life in order to produce faith, He will do it. He will then exercise His full sovereignty which will produce optimum growth in you. At times there will be difficult and costly lessons. Nonetheless, He will be in full control of every event.

On the other hand, if you resist Him in the area of faith—or if you are simply not interested in growth—He will not force you against your will. He then will not fully exercise His sovereignty for your benefit. He is still sovereign because your free moral agency is the result of His creative work. But you will not benefit from what He could do for you because, by your choice, you have denied His offer to exercise His sovereignty on your behalf.

———————  •  ———————

# *10* Faith and Holiness

There is a fundamental change you must make when you determine to live by faith. *You can no longer depend on organized religious institutions as a functional substitute[1] for personal dependence on God.*

If you want to live by faith, you must be in direct communication with Almighty God Himself, and then pattern your life after *His* holiness. You can no longer measure your life according to the standards held by your Christian peers. You must take personal responsibility for establishing your own standard of holy living.

•

God initiated four specific areas of growth in my Christian life. I have already mentioned the first three:

1. *A foundation of knowing Jesus as Almighty, Sovereign, Creator God.*
2. *The desire to ask Jesus to give me a deep love for Him.*
3. *The desire to ask Jesus to give me an implicit trust (faith) in Him.*

The final area of growth was,

4. *The desire to ask Jesus to make me a godly man even when I have no innate desire for holiness.*

In the same way I have prayed for both faith and a love for Jesus, I have also prayed that God would produce holiness in my life. I regard the three requests of loving Jesus, trusting Jesus, and being a godly man as the essential elements in my relationship with Him. All other things—including ministry—are secondary issues that will grow out of these three.

I have described these benchmarks in my own life because I think they are biblically relevant. God, however, will lead you uniquely.

•

---

[1] A *functional substitute* is an institution that replaces another primary institution when that primary institution becomes inaccessible or unresponsive, or is held in low esteem. As used above, *dependence on organized religious institutions* (to provide direction in your life) replaces *personal dependence on God*. *Functional substitutes* will be discussed more completely in Chapter 18.

Ephesians 1:4 states God's earliest purpose for our being:

[God] chose us in [Jesus Christ] before the foundation of the world, that we should be holy and blameless before Him (NASB).

Before God began creating the cosmos, He determined that He would choose for Himself people who possessed His absolute holiness. Of course, we now understand that this holiness is only available through faith in Jesus. But the earliest demand of Almighty God is, nonetheless, that we as believers are to be holy and blameless, meeting the same standard God holds for Himself.

His standard is not relative to our standing in human society. The holiness He demands is His own absolute standard of holiness.

In Matthew 5:48 Jesus said,

"Therefore you are to be perfect, as your heavenly Father is perfect." (NASB)

Nothing less is satisfactory to Him.

•

Scripture clearly identifies the believer living in today's world as one who is called to live a holy (godly) life.

Once you were alienated from God and were enemies in your minds because of your evil behavior. But now he has reconciled you by Christ's physical body through death to present you holy in his sight, without blemish and free from accusation—if you continue in your faith, established and firm, not moved from the hope held out in the gospel (Colossians 1:21-23).

As obedient children, do not be conformed to [your] former lusts...but like the Holy One who called you, be holy yourselves also in all your behavior; because it is written, "You shall be holy, for I am holy" (I Peter 1:14-16 NASB).

•

A pursuit of holiness will include the following:

1. A high standard of obedience toward God.

Offer yourselves to God...you are slaves to the one whom you obey—whether you are slaves to sin, which leads to death, or to obedience, which leads to righteousness (Romans 6:13, 16).

2. Holiness as a frequent and intense subject of prayer.

But, you man of God...pursue righteousness, godliness, faith, love, endurance and gentleness (I Timothy 6:11).

Flee the evil desires of youth, and pursue righteousness, faith, love and peace (2 Tim. 2:22).

3. A disciplined life that avoids sin.

Therefore do not let sin reign in your mortal body....Do not offer the parts of your body to sin, as instruments of wickedness, but rather offer yourselves to God, as those who have been brought from death to life; and offer the parts of your body to him as instruments of righteousness (Romans 6:12-13).

•

Biblical holiness is often mistaken for *moral* or *religious* behavior. It is neither. Moral behavior is commendable, but it is a learned human response. Religious[2] behavior apart from the work of God is perverse because it adopts creeds and standards of behavior as functional substitutes for the work of God in a believer's life. *True holiness is a reflection of God's perfect nature manifested in the believer's life.* It cannot be counterfeited by human effort.

•

For the majority of believers, there is probably no greater hindrance to a life of prayer and godliness in today's society than television, video, and cinema entertainment. Let me simply relate my own perspective without suggesting that it is more than my personal standard.

I almost never watch television. We have not had a TV in our home for many years. This is an admission of personal weakness, not strength. I become engrossed in anything I do, and therefore find it difficult to turn off a program after I've begun watching it. However, *it has been my personal experience that television watching of any kind has an immediate and noticeably dulling effect on my prayer life.* It isn't simply that watching TV robs me of prayer time. The vitality of my prayer life diminishes immediately.

We must avoid moralistic pronouncements that deny something —television programming in this case—because it is "evil." We need to dig deeper and carefully evaluate the core issues. (In this discussion I am considering only the content of *entertainment programming*—not *educational programming*. In addition, television

---

2 James 1:27 talks about "pure and undefiled religion" which pleases God. Religious behavior which merely adopts creeds and standards of behavior as functional substitutes for the work of God is, however, contrary to biblical Christianity and is therefore perverse.

*technology* is amoral; it can be used for either good or evil.)

Romans 1 has a direct application to a core issue regarding media entertainment. After listing what he has described as "every kind of wickedness, evil, greed and depravity" in the earlier part of the chapter, Paul says:

> Although [those who have practiced evil] know God's righteous decree that those who do such things deserve death, they not only continue to do those very things *but also approve of those who practice them* (verse 32). (Emphasis added.)

Paul is describing an amphitheater crowd cheering on those who are practicing evil. Even when they are not doing evil themselves, the crowd is vicariously enjoying watching others flaunt evil. In Paul's description, the cheering comes from spectators in Satan's stadium. Today, the cheering comes from the living rooms of professing Christians who are able to applaud without going to the arena. I must ask myself this question, "If sin is so heinous that Jesus gave His life to free me from its bondage, what happens to me when I vicariously enjoy that which He died to save me from?" *There is no way I can take delight in what Jesus hates without seriously eroding my relationship to the One I profess to love.*

There is another core issue that comes closer to the present topic of holiness. When one begins to pursue godly living, there is a natural gravitation toward holiness and avoidance of sin. This does not occur merely because we are coerced to avoid sin, but because we genuinely "hunger and thirst for righteousness" (Matthew 5:6). While we are pursuing godliness, something is happening inside which internally motivates us to *want* to avoid contamination from sin. Said in another way, while pursuing godliness, we are moving in the direction of asking, "How can I arrange to encounter less sin?" The opposite response is *required* when we watch most of television's entertainment programming. The viewer must constantly be asking, "How much sin can I tolerate before I must change channels?" *You simply cannot be asking the latter question and expect to grow in godliness. It is impossible.*

I am aghast at the naiveté of the Christian television, video, and cinema audience. Obscenity, profanity and explicit sexuality are far from the primary objectionable issues in modern entertainment programming. Jesus didn't die just to save me from hearing certain words. He died to save me from a *value system* that idealizes wealth, physical attractiveness and prowess, deceitfulness, unfaithfulness in marriage, independence from absolute moral authority, and all of the other misplaced values that are routinely portrayed in programming and advertising. (Notice "and advertising.") When evaluating programs for their children, Christian parents often fall into a predictable trap. They make an effort to screen programming for objectionable language and sexual content without giving consideration to the *value systems* being taught. *We cannot willingly submerge ourselves in an unbiblical value system and not have it negatively affect our spiritual growth.*

•

This last section has been candid. However, considering the excesses of the Christian community today, it is an issue that both our lay people and our leaders must seriously evaluate. God demands holiness. We cannot expect to develop a life of faith without dealing severely with our natural human appetite for sin.

•

Someone may observe that believers could not live in the real world if they were so fragile that watching television programs containing offensive language and negative value systems would cripple them spiritually. The answer has to do with our responsibility to make personal choices.

For more than 20 years I have purposely worked in the secular world and I frequently hear offensive language. When I start a new job, I take personal responsibility for the kind of calendars hanging in *my* workspace and I am meticulously careful of my own speech. Though I never reprimand others for their foul language, in time other employees will occasionally correct their offensive language when they are around me. There are times when I simply walk away from conversations or avoid working with certain individuals because I don't want to hear the trash. I believe it can be appropriate for us as believers to work in a profane environment with the intent of living a godly life and bearing witness to the work of God in our lives. *If God has directed us in this decision, I believe that we can trust the Spirit to protect our minds in those situations that are outside of our control.*

That is very different from *choosing* to expose ourselves to the same profanity, obscenity and sexually explicit programming in our entertainment. Said somewhat facetiously, I expect the Spirit to protect my mind when I am engaged in spiritual warfare in the workplace for His sake. I do *not* presume on His protection of my mind when I am watching television; He has given me a will controlled by spiritual judgment. In addition, there is an "off" button He expects me to use. *Protection of my mind as I sit in front of a television set is my responsibility.*

•

What has been said about television could equally be applied to reading. For some believers, pulp novels, checkout counter tabloids, and other reading choices become a powerful deterrent to growth in Christ.

•

Godliness is not a burden the believer must bear. Our redemption will result in a life that is satisfying in every respect. It is one of Satan's great deceptions that holiness is drudgery. In eternity, we will find that reflecting God's holiness is a wonderful satisfaction. We can experience that same delight in this life as well.

Blessed are those who hunger and thirst for righteousness, for they shall be satisfied (Matthew 5:6 NASB).

•

In light of my closing suggestion, we need to be careful that we do not adopt what is often called *legalism.* Holiness is *not* self-denial or asceticism. It is not living by rules that identify certain things that we cannot do.

Legalism is just as repugnant to God—and as detrimental to a life of faith—as is living in known sin. It, too, is merely a self-effort of works.

Under no circumstances does legalism precede living by faith.

•

I believe that the issue of holiness will be the deciding factor in the success or failure of the decision of many readers to live by faith.

You may decide that you will begin praying for faith, and then discipline yourself to spend the necessary time in extended prayer. You may be willing to face what comes by way of adversity in order to grow by faith. You may decide that, if God directs, you will make your time and your finances wholly available to Him.

But if you attempt to compromise in the area of holiness, Satan will "devour" you.

I cannot tell you that either media entertainment or certain types of reading are forbidden to you. That is God's prerogative. Yet, I can well imagine that even though you are willing to make every other sacrifice to live by faith, you may justify involvement in this one area.

Before the foundation of the world, God chose us to be holy and blameless before Him. He still holds us to the same standard of righteousness to which He holds Himself. Certainly, this is through the imputed righteousness of Jesus, and allows for the continued necessity of confessed sin. But we cannot willfully compromise His work of producing holiness in our lives and still expect to live by faith.

I would give you this counsel. If you are serious in your intent to live by faith, plan to refrain from any media entertainment for at least one year. If you live alone—or can reach agreement with your spouse—remove all TV sets from your home. If there are others in the family who would object, then have them move the TV into their own room. (Do not insist that other family members follow your example unless it is their own choice to do so.) Finally, I would suggest that you eliminate media entertainment *before* you begin pursuing faith.

Holiness in regard to media entertainment may be the single most difficult issue you will face in learning to live by faith.

# *11* Faith and Adversity

There are two fundamental issues which make some degree of adversity inevitable for mankind in general, and believers in particular. Understanding why we encounter adversity will help us as we learn to live by faith.

## Adversity is normal

As a result of sin, all of creation is flawed. In spite of that reality, both Western culture and the Western Church are essentially hedonistic. They both expect life to be *good* and they search for an explanation when it isn't. The truth is just the opposite. We are sinful men and women and we live in a world that is corrupted by sin. Until creation's future redemption occurs as promised in Romans 8:20-21, our lives will always be subject to hardship. We should express social concern and a willingness to alleviate suffering. Nonetheless, adversity to one degree or another is common to mankind.

While we are living in this world as believers, we must understand that adversity in our personal lives is not necessarily an indication of God's judgment. In a general sense, adversity is merely the context in which we live. God's sovereignty acts on our behalf within this context of our fallen world.

## Adversity produces growth

There is a specific purpose for adversity that both our Western culture and our Western Church also want to deny. History gives countless examples of people who have experienced substantial personal growth as a result of extreme hardship.

This is even more true for the believer who wants to live by faith. James 1:2-5 says:

> Consider it pure joy, my brothers, whenever you face trials of many kinds, because you know that the testing of your faith develops perseverance. Perseverance must finish its work so that you may be mature and complete, not lacking anything. If any of you lacks wisdom, he should ask God, who gives generously to all without finding fault, and it will be given to him.

•

In spite of all of the difficulty diabetes has caused in my life, I am deeply grateful to God for allowing me to live as a diabetic for 35 years. No other physical circumstance in my life has contributed more to my spiritual growth than my diabetes.

My first lessons concerning the sovereignty of God, my recognition of my mortality and the need to think realistically about death, the need to define my personal position regarding reliance on medicine, my understanding of my responsibility to use time wisely because I may not have a normal life expectancy, and many lessons in faith have all resulted from living with this disease. By nature, I am an independent and self-reliant individual. I could dread what the future holds for me as my health continues to deteriorate. On the other hand, as I risk losing my eyesight, my driver's license, my overall health, and especially my income, I am also increasingly aware of Jesus' ability to sustain me. I understand that all of these health issues are His wonderful provision to my prayer for faith.

I have asked intently for faith. Jesus has given me diabetes—and several other persistently difficult areas in my life—so that my faith may grow. Even from the perspective of this life, I am thankful for that growth. In the future, when I look back from the vantage point of Heaven, I will realize even more how wonderfully He planned my life so that I could learn to trust Him.

•

I often marvel at the public prayers of Christians. Week after week in the adult Bible study class I attend, I hear prayer asking God's deliverance from impending hardships.

I wonder how God must react when He carefully plans an event in a believer's life for the purpose of promoting growth in faith, only to hear the Sunday morning group asking Him to change His mind because this or that believer doesn't really want to learn that lesson. (The disturbing thing is that no one ever suggests that these trials are likely God's provision for growth.) Does God ever shake His head in dismay at what He hears us asking for?

I don't want to imply that it is not appropriate to bring health needs or other areas of difficulty to Him in prayer. It most certainly is. But I think the emphasis of the request should be the growth of the one involved while also recognizing God's sovereignty in that believer's life.

# *12* Matthew 6:19-34 for Today

These verses deal with the real life issues of accumulating wealth and caring for our physical needs. Yet there is something even more basic underlying these verses. Jesus is asking us to review our *priorities*.

Your felt needs in earning a living and working toward professional advancement reflect your priorities. On the simplest level, you must decide whether you will place the highest importance on earning enough money for your perceived needs, or if you will place the highest priority on trusting Jesus for your future.

There are two issues at stake. The first considers our resources of time and energy, and the second considers our perception of need. In the first case, we must recognize our finite resources. We have only a limited amount of time, physical energy, and emotional drive, and we can only *spend* it once. Our priority will determine whether we invest our resources for ourselves or for Jesus.

The second issue is our *perception* of need. Our society and the sub-groups to which we belong (including our Christian sub-culture) condition us to have certain expectations of both present and future need. These perceived needs may or may not be *true* needs. After much preparation for health, retirement years and so on, God may lead in a direction that bypasses our perceived needs. For example, an early death may eliminate future financial needs, or His way of providing for them may be entirely different than what we expected. Our perception of what we will need in the future may be quite different from how God actually intends to provide for us.

Consider the issue of priorities in Matthew 6:24:

"No one can serve two masters. Either he will hate the one and love the other, or he will be devoted to the one and despise the other. You cannot serve both God and Money.

Jesus is not saying that a believer should not work to earn a living. He is emphasizing a limitation of the finite human mind. We cannot establish two parallel yet conflicting priorities. Given the same finite resources of time and energy, we cannot have equal priorities of gaining wealth and serving God. We must give one a place of priority while letting the other become secondary. If we choose to put serving God first, we must entrust Him with the consequences of that decision. If we choose to make earning an income or advancing professionally our first priority, we have relegated serving God to a subordinate position.

The fact that you have a secular job does not necessarily mean that earning money is your highest priority. Many believers have successfully used secular incomes to enable them to serve Jesus, having purposefully restricted their employment so that it becomes a means to this end. Ultimately, only you will know your own motivation.

Nor does Christian employment confirm that God has been given the highest priority. There is ample opportunity to *serve money* in full-time Christian service. A pastor may hesitate to confront sin or a lack of zeal in his congregation in order to avoid jeopardizing his salary. It is a common practice for older individuals in full-time ministries to continue working in order to qualify for retirement benefits even when they are no longer effective. There is also much opportunity to *serve money* in the huge business enterprise associated with selling Christian books and merchandise and speaking or performing publicly.

Consider this example of priorities. Let's say that your physician recommends that you begin taking a certain medication because studies show that it reduces the death rate. You are now faced with a very simple issue of priorities. You can trust medical science to prolong your life, or you can trust Jesus to give—or take—your life as He pleases.[1]

Say that you decide to take the medication without first praying about it. Then say that the medication actually prolongs your life by four years. *Would four years of additional life be of greater value to you in Heaven than living the remainder of eternity with the knowledge that you did not trust Jesus in this area?*

I have personally decided that I must always make decisions based upon what will be best for me in Heaven rather than what appears to be best here on earth. I am a fallible human being with imperfect knowledge and judgment. Yet, after I get to Heaven, I will always be more satisfied looking back on my imperfect human

---

[1] I am artificially making this example one in which you must choose one of only two options. A third possible option would be that God could certainly lead you to use medication even though you were fully trusting Him. (See the qualification to *conventional means* and *primary recourse* in Chapter 1.) Nonetheless, I am giving the example as having only two options because I want you to understand that, at times, God may give you an opportunity to act in faith in exactly this way.

decisions that were based on faith in Jesus rather than on those based on my trust in human institutions.

•

How willing are you to take Jesus' teaching in Matthew 6 literally? How do you want to account for your responses when you stand before Him in Heaven?

"Do not store up for yourselves treasures on earth, where moth and rust destroy, and where thieves break in and steal. But store up for yourselves treasures in heaven, where moth and rust do not destroy, and where thieves do not break in and steal. For where your treasure is, there your heart will be also[2] (19-22).

"Therefore I tell you, do not worry about your life, what you will eat or drink; or about your body, what you will wear. Is not life more important than food, and the body more important than clothes? Look at the birds of the air; they do not sow or reap or store away in barns, and yet your heavenly Father feeds them. Are you not much more valuable than they? Who of you by worrying can add a single hour to his life?

"And why do you worry about clothes? See how the lilies of the field grow. They do not labor or spin. Yet I tell you that not even Solomon in all his splendor was dressed like one of these. If that is how God clothes the grass of the field, which is here today and tomorrow is thrown into the fire, will he not much more clothe you, O you of little faith? So do not worry, saying, 'What shall we eat?' or 'What shall we drink?' or 'What shall we wear?' For the pagans run after all these things, and your heavenly Father knows that you need them. But seek first his kingdom and his righteousness, and all these things will be given to you as well. Therefore do not worry about tomorrow, for tomorrow will worry about itself. Each day has enough trouble of its own" (25-34).

These verses represent a high standard for anyone contemplating living by faith. Jesus expects us to trust God rather than our own resources for our essential needs in life. Are you willing to ask for His direction in this area of living by faith?

•

I often carry a small New Testament in my lunch box. For three or

---

2 Have you ever had the thrill of realizing that you are truly living as though your treasure *is* in Heaven? Have you ever become aware that you are genuinely more concerned with your investments for Jesus' sake than you are about expenditures for your own well-being?

four months this past year I repeatedly read these same verses from Matthew 6 during my lunch hour. It is a thought-provoking passage. Was Jesus just talking to some simple peasants who had little to lose anyway? Maybe it is just hyperbole. Maybe Jesus just wants me to work a little harder at my Sunday Christian activities! Besides that, it's obvious that I have to do my part in working for a living.

Or did Jesus really mean what He said? Is Jesus telling me that if I will put His interests first, the Father will take special care of me?

"But Jesus, do you know that my health is failing and that I need to build as much retirement as possible? I may soon be unemployable. I may lose my eyesight. Jesus, I am afraid. Can I really trust that what you said is true for me today? What if I put your interests first and the Father doesn't take care of me when I need it...?"

# *13* Using Faith in Prayer

Prayer is a verbal expression of faith. Faith is not a vague sense of well-being, but is specific reliance on God to *do* something (which was described as *acting* faith), or to *be* something in our need (described as *resting* faith). Prayer is a means of defining our expectation of what God will *do* or *be*.

By its very nature, living by faith will involve a well-developed prayer life.

### The Most Holy Place of prayer

Hebrews 10:19-22 paints an interesting picture of prayer:

> Therefore, brothers, *since we have confidence to enter the Most Holy Place by the blood of Jesus*, by a new and living way *opened for us through the curtain*, that is, his body, and since we have a great priest over the house of God, let us draw near to God with a sincere heart in full assurance of faith. (Emphasis added.)

Herod the Great built the Temple in Jerusalem that was in use during Jesus' lifetime. The single building which was the Temple proper consisted of an enclosed *Porch*, the *Holy Place*, and the *Most Holy Place*. A double curtain separated the *Holy Place* from the *Most Holy Place*. (See Figure 6 on the next page.) The *Holy Place* contained the altar of incense, the table of showbread, and the lampstand. Only the officiating priests could enter this first room. They brought in the morning and evening incense, trimmed the lamps daily, and replaced the showbread every Sabbath. The second room, the *Most Holy Place*, had no furnishings. (Prior to the fall of Jerusalem, the *Most Holy Place* in Solomon's Temple contained the Ark of the Covenant.) It was here that the Glory of God resided. Only the High Priest could enter the *Most Holy Place*, and that but once a year after offering sacrifice and making careful preparation. The Temple proper was not a public meeting place.

The double curtain between the *Holy Place* and the *Most Holy Place* formed a labyrinth. The curtain was oriented north-to-south. The High Priest would enter at the south side of the curtain (entering from the *Holy Place*) and thread his way through the narrow passage between the two curtains, emerging into the *Most Holy Place* from the north end of the curtain. Scripture refers to this double curtain assemblage as a curtain or *veil*.

The *Temple* in Jesus' time included not only the Temple proper, but a number of courtyards and dividing walls. There was a large courtyard surrounding the central Temple structure that Gentiles could enter. In the center of this *Court of the Gentiles*, a smaller walled courtyard called the *Women's Court*, was provided for both Jewish men and women. Only devout Jewish men could pass through the *Women's Court* and then enter the innermost *Court of Israel*. The Temple building itself stood in the center of the restricted *Court of Israel*. As shown in Figure 6, the Temple structure included an outdoor platform on which both the *Altar for Burnt Offerings* and the Temple proper were located. Entrance into the Temple *Porch* was through an outer curtain.

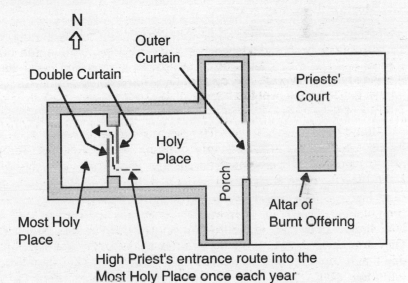

Figure 6   The Curtain (or Veil) in the Temple of Jesus' day which separated the Holy Place from the Most Holy Place. This was the curtain which was torn from top to bottom when Jesus died.

Something amazing happened at the moment Jesus died. *The double curtain that separated the Most Holy Place from the Holy Place was torn from top to bottom* (Matthew 27:51). At three o'clock on Friday afternoon, this room that no man could see on pain of death, was suddenly exposed. That it was directly connected to Jesus' death was undeniable.

One can imagine what may have happened next. It may have been one of the most humorous incidents in all of Scripture. The Sabbath was to start in about three hours. After sundown, all work would be prohibited. How to clear the men's inner courtyard of all curious bystanders, how to get this curtain temporarily repaired so that the Sabbath sacrifices could resume, how to stop the priests who had been in the area from saying too much, and how to get it all done in three hours must have caused untold consternation. And all of this was taking place on the important Passover Sabbath when Jerusalem was filled with expatriate Jews! Can you imagine the almost comical spectacle of these weary Sanhedrin members who had been awake all Thursday night conducting Jesus' trials, trying to direct repairs to the damage without setting foot inside the sacred room?

Do you revel in your "confidence to enter the Most Holy Place by the blood of Jesus, by a new and living way opened for us through the curtain, that is, his body" (Hebrews 10:19-20)? Can you imagine what it must have been like for an officiating priest standing in the *Porch* or *Holy Place* on that Friday afternoon to see the curtain torn in two and to then be exposed to the area where the Glory of God resided? He would have been gripped with overpowering fear, expecting to die immediately. *Do we have any appreciation for what it means to be able to boldly enter into the Most Holy Place ourselves and directly petition Almighty God?*

In prayer, I often visualize myself in the *Most Holy Place*. In that Place, I have direct access to Almighty God. There is no time limit to meet. I can come as frequently as I want and stay as long as I like. "Let us draw near to God with a sincere heart in full assurance of faith" (Hebrews 10:22). But I want to use my privileged time well. I don't dare be frivolous. I want to ask Him for things that please Him, and I also want to ask Him to do things that only He can accomplish. I want to take full advantage of that privilege for His sake, for my sake, and for the sake of ministry.

How do you spend *your* time in the *Most Holy Place*?

## The Spirit's help in prayer

As fallible human beings, we cannot possibly know what God wants to ultimately accomplish in each thing we might pray about. We have general guidelines in Scripture, but explicit instruction for praying about a specific need is usually lacking.

God has provided a wonderful and practical solution to this

problem. Romans 8:25-27 says,

> But if we hope for what we do not yet have, we wait for it patiently. In the same way, the Spirit helps us in our weakness. We do not know what we ought to pray for, but the Spirit himself intercedes for us with groans that words cannot express. And he who searches our hearts knows the mind of the Spirit, because the Spirit intercedes for the saints in accordance with God's will.

The Spirit does two things for us in prayer. First, He intercedes for us so that even though we might not know how best to state our request, the Spirit molds our request into a form that God can answer. At some time, most of us have prayed intently for something and then have seen our prayer answered in a more perfect way than we had imagined. It was clear that God had heard and answered our prayer, but it was also evident that He did it in His own way rather than according to our inadequate request. This, I believe, is the work of the Spirit in taking that request and molding it so that it becomes a viable and answerable petition.

Secondly, the Spirit may actually reveal to us specific details regarding a request. He may show us *what* to pray for as well as setting other guidelines so that the form of the request is exactly what He intends to answer.[1] I believe it is appropriate to select major topics that we want to pray about without knowing precisely *what* we will be requesting. In the initial stages, we may pray generally for the topic but spend considerably more time praying for specific direction as to what we should request. Subsequently, after He shows us His will, we can then ask God very specifically for what we believe He will do in response to our faith.

There is a wonderful opportunity to grow in faith through this process of asking the Spirit to define precise areas of prayer. At the same time, we must avoid overconfidence and reliance on our own strength and wisdom. We must also avoid presuming on God and demanding that He reveal His will to us. In many cases, it is *not* His will that we should know how He intends to answer our prayer.

Be sensitive to God's leading and use the opportunity for growth in faith. At the same time, be cautious and aware of your own fallibility before Almighty God.

•

---

[1] Read a biography of J.O. Fraser for an example of this type of prayer in his request for the salvation of the Lisu people in China. (*Mountain Rain*, by Eileen Fraser Crossman, or *Behind the Ranges* by Mrs. Howard Taylor.)

One of the capacities of the human mind is its ability to gain insight concerning an unsolved problem through the process of discussion. This same capacity of the mind can be used in prayer.

Often, the process of praying about something will give further insight into how to proceed in prayer for that need. Allow the Spirit to use this human faculty to direct you in prayer. In the early stages of praying for a new topic, bring the need to God while acknowledging that you are uncertain what you should request. Then allow Him to remold your request into that which He actually wants to accomplish. Do not be afraid to see your request change significantly from what you first prayed for.

## Our approach in prayer

We need to briefly evaluate prayer formats. Generally, when you read biographies of men or women who have spent much time in prayer, you will see that they used some form of a notebook with lists of items and individuals needing prayer. Typically, you will also read of them making notations of answered prayer.

Personally, much as I can understand the "efficiency" of prayer notebooks, I have tried this method numerous times and have always abandoned it as being too mechanical.[2] (Presently, I am trying to keep a list that I occasionally use, but I spend most of my time in less structured prayer.)

If you are just beginning to spend concentrated time in prayer, let me make the following suggestions. First, don't adopt a format that will make prayer drudgery for you, irrespective of its presumed efficiency. Secondly, place the emphasis on time spent with Jesus rather than on requests for ministry or people.

•

Have you ever attempted to pray without an agenda? You will need both privacy and ample unstructured time. (My formal[3] prayer

---

[2] To be honest, my problem may simply be that it takes more energy! There is nothing objectionable about reading prayers whether they are from the Psalms or other Scripture, meaningful liturgical prayers, or ones we ourselves have written which express the depth of our supplication.

[3] I am defining *formal* prayer as planned prayer time, which—for me—is done while kneeling. (A number of years ago, to spare my knees, I began using a single pillow my young daughter made for me as a gift. Then I needed two thick pillows. Now I use a slanted board placed between the floor and the chair with a large pillow that I can lay on. My knees have had enough!) In

time while kneeling is done in the evening because this fits my schedule best. I generally use this prayer format on evenings when I will not be working the following day. At least once a week I like to spend two to four hours or more in a single prayer time.)

To pray without an agenda, you go before God, saying in effect, "I will be here for the next two hours. I want to enjoy being with You, but I don't have many things I plan to ask You for. I will let *You* be responsible for what happens; if You want, you can bring specific thoughts and requests to my mind."

There can be a great advantage in allowing longer blocks of time for prayer. If I have a sense of restlessness and futility in prayer, it is almost always in the first part of the prayer time. After I have been praying for 45 minutes, it is likely that I will enjoyably continue praying for another hour or two. And yes, there *are* times when I quit early simply because the time is not producing satisfactory results.

There are times when prayer without an agenda becomes intense, and I leave my prayer time feeling exhilarated. On the other hand, last night was an example of the extreme opposite. I "prayed" for almost four hours, but this morning as I am writing, I can remember little that took place. Nor can I even relate to having had a sense of awe from being in the Presence of God. When I finally left my study, I was groggy and most certainly had slept during my prayer time.

I tell you this because unrealistic expectations will certainly hinder your prayer life. My prayer time is always worthwhile, but to say the least, it is not always intense.

•

I more frequently pray by "waiting on God" for a certain request. As an outgrowth of my prayer for faith, God has given me a specific ministry that has an element of absolute impossibility from a human perspective. Even though I have spent many hours *laboring* in this ministry, I am acutely aware that my effort will have no effect unless God does the work.

As a result, I have spent many extended times praying while "waiting on God" regarding this area of ministry. Even though there are many requests I can—and do—make, I will often acknowledge to Jesus that I am coming to Him as an advocate for the group of people I am praying for. During that "waiting" time, many petitions certainly come to mind. Equally important, however, is the sense

---

contrast, *spontaneous* prayer may occur anytime during the day or while lying awake at night.

that I have entered the *Most Holy Place* in behalf of those people because of their need. The issue is not the *number* of requests I bring to God, but the act of holding the need of these people before Him for that period of time.

There is no esoteric power in the prayer format I have just described. Nonetheless, I believe that the Spirit can use this "waiting" time to bring requests to mind, as well as developing in me the commitment to take the enormity of the task seriously, acknowledging the need for God Himself to act.

## Time and prayer

The person who spends little time in prayer typically finds prayer difficult and laborious. This individual will rarely pray *spontaneously.* In contrast, when your prayer life and love for Jesus grow, you will find an increasing enjoyment and desire to pray. As your *formal* prayer life grows, you will find an increasing delight and frequency in *spontaneous* prayer as well. I have discovered *recreational* prayer; I pray because I *enjoy* it.

•

We *must* start our life by faith with a desire to love Jesus. Unless this is something you have already spent considerable time pursuing, *make your love for Jesus your first area of concentrated prayer.* What will you need to do if you want to pursue loving Him? Logically, *the emphasis will be on spending time with Jesus, rather than merely reciting a long list of requests.*

Use this subject as the foundation for extended prayer. Try "waiting on God" regarding your love for Jesus.

•

As your faith grows, your prayer life will also grow. Prayer is an important vehicle for responding in faith. However, this does not imply that faith precedes prayer. Just as we may learn more about prayer through the process of growing in faith, so we may learn more about faith by practicing prayer. Each will have a positive influence on the other.

If you want to learn to live by faith, you will also need to make provision for a more effective prayer life. You will need to set aside specific time for prayer. Your prayer life will need to become a high priority for you.

———————  •  ———————

# *14* Using Faith in Everyday Life

You will miss God's purpose for your life of faith if you believe that the primary purpose of faith is to accomplish ministry. It is not! The reason God wants you to learn to live by faith is so that your everyday life will please Him as you trust Him daily.

If you work in the trades, then it is in the context of your life as a plumber, a cement mason, a mechanical contractor, or whatever else, that He wants to see you live by faith. If you are a professional, then it is at your receptionist's desk, in your office cubicle, at your CAD drafting station, at your hospital or within the professional context of your work where your life of faith must be lived.

Each of us also has responsibilities within our family and community life as well as other obligations and leisure activities that comprise our life. These are also the areas in which God wants us to live by faith.

•

Any area of your work or personal life in which you must make decisions is an area in which you may apply faith. If you own your own business, there will be countless times in which you will find that living by faith will require a business ethic different than the accepted norm. You will need to rely heavily on God when you take risks because of your desire to honor Him.

Family finances, children's schooling, retirement living, or insurance coverage will also be areas of decision that give ample opportunity to exercise faith.

•

Living by faith is an all-encompassing way of life. You will not be able to compartmentalize ministry as something requiring faith, while personal finances and similar areas are done without faith. If you are intent on pursuing faith, it will touch every area of your life.

•

In all probability, God will not deal *simultaneously* with every potential faith issue in your life.

———————  •  ———————

# *15* Using Faith in Ministry

When you begin pursuing faith, God will most likely lead you into ministries which will require faith.

•

In this book, I am using the term *ministry* to mean:

Christian service which: 1) is the result of God's direction, and 2) has the primary objective of benefiting other people rather than institutions or yourself.

This definition doesn't focus on the *activity* as much as it does on the *motivation.* For example, you may become a parent volunteer in your child's classroom. If you are doing it merely because you enjoy children and are building skills for possible future employment, it is not ministry. On the other hand, if you are doing it for those same reasons, but you also determine before God that it is at His direction and that you want to influence others for the Gospel, then it becomes ministry. The underlying theme of *motivation* evaluates the activity as being *Christian service,* at *God's direction,* and as something that *primarily benefits other people* rather than yourself or institutions and facilities. Again, motivation enters into the definition. If you are working on a building project so that you will get time-share in a beach vacation cabin, it isn't ministry. If you are working on a building project because others will benefit in some way, it may be a viable ministry in either a Christian or secular context.

I am not defining ministry in a technical sense. I am merely emphasizing that ministry is an activity you undertake at God's direction for the benefit of other people. Obviously, you could be involved in something that was not ministry when it first started, but developed into ministry as a result of further planning. Equally, something could cease to be ministry that had begun as such.

•

Many activities that are identified as *ministry* in Christian circles have little to do with faith. Frequently, they are merely activities used to maintain the tradition of that institution. However, even in these settings you may be able to have an excellent ministry. Much will depend on your own viewpoint and purpose as to whether you are seeking a true ministry or merely becoming a custodian of institutional tradition.

•

In some areas of ministry, the requirement for faith will be obvious. You may undertake a ministry in which people are overtly resistant to the Gospel or one in which the growth of other Christians has been stifled.

Other ministries may seem less demanding. These may be existing ministries that already have strong spiritual leadership.

In either case, God can lead you into very personal and unexpected areas of faith. Faith may focus on the need of a particular individual within the ministry. Faith may cause you to focus on a weakness in your own life. Faith may also focus on the leadership or the institution itself.

•

Earlier, I said that as you live by faith, the direction for your life will increasingly come from your time spent with Jesus and less from Christian institutions. This direction may be as simple as a decision to befriend an unbelieving secular co-worker. On the other hand, your life of faith may lead you into ministries that will result in heavy time and financial commitments.

In these new ministry ventures you must be particularly wise as you pray about God's direction. Learn how to appropriately seek counsel from others. However, there will also be times when the very individuals from whom you would logically seek counsel are the ones most in need of change. There may be times when your life of faith will lead you into solitary decisions. (I am intrigued by the response given to William Carey by his own ministerial association. Carey—who is now known as the Father of Modern Missions—was admonished after a presentation in which he advocated foreign missions. The moderator said to him, "Young man, sit down! You are an enthusiast. When God pleases to converse with heathen He'll do it without consulting you or me."[1] Carey went to India in 1793 and successfully translated Scripture into many Indian and Burmese languages. But his lifetime of ministry was dogged by isolation, misunderstanding, and numerous financial and personal failures.)

•

My personal experience may give an illustration regarding the sequence of faith and ministry. For many years I was active in public

---

[1] *William Carey,* by Basil Miller, Bethany House Publishers, page 32.

ministry roles. None of them, however, involved high risk or more than "conventional" faith. This was true even in the early years after I first began praying for faith.

As I mentioned in an earlier chapter, I began watching other believers who had a "bigger" God than I did. I wanted to see Him work in my life as well. I began asking God to increase my faith, and if possible, to show me evidence of His power.

One evening God seemed to respond by giving me a choice. I must be cautious since the impression may simply have come from my own imagination. (This is not said to discredit God's ability to lead; it is merely recognition of my human limitations.) In asking God to increase my faith, I was asking Him to do much more in me than I had allowed Him to do previously. I believe He gave me a specific choice between one of two things He would do in order to show His might. Either He would heal me of my diabetes, or He would bring to Himself a group of people for whom I had been praying with my "conventional" faith.

My choice was made without hesitation. Healing would merely benefit *me* and would be only a menial task for the Creator. However, if God would grant my other request, the consequences would resound throughout eternity because of its magnitude. Without being specific, I can assure you that it was then—and remains so today—a humanly impossible task. Without question, I wanted Him to do the latter.

This request has not yet been answered almost 5 years later. I may not see the answer in my lifetime. But I can see evidence that God is working!

Since that time, I have faced intense spiritual warfare. There has been immensely high cost to me in the ministry He gave me as well as in other areas such as my health. However, both my faith and a resulting prayer ministry have grown significantly.

I related the above story in order to suggest an answer to the question, "Which comes first, faith or ministry?" Certainly, in my own experience, some viable ministry preceded my pursuit of faith. There is no doubt in my mind, however, that faith has resulted in a vastly increased ministry for me.

If you want to have an effective ministry, pursue faith. As your faith grows, God can entrust you with more strategic ministries.

●

By no means is ministry limited to public activity. In fact, you may find that the more you are able to live by faith, the more God removes you from public ministry. My own experience cannot be taken as a standard, because God deals uniquely with each individual. Nonetheless, God has increasingly taken me out of active public ministries of leadership and Bible teaching and led me into ministries that are out of public view.

•

Prayer will become an important part of your life of faith. You may increasingly experience the strategic importance of prayer in doing God's work. I hope you do!

The contemporary evangelical Church has gone through a span of almost forty years in which there has been increasing emphasis on better theological training for clergy and greater organization for institutional ministries. Concurrently, however, the emphasis on prayer has waned. Thankfully, I believe this situation is changing with a new emphasis on prayer among these same churches.

God may call you to a ministry of prayer either as the primary portion of your ministry or as a complement to your existing ministry. As the believer who is living by faith ages or faces increasing physical limitations, prayer offers continued ministry opportunities until the moment of death.

•

J. O. Fraser went to China as a missionary in 1908. His work in taking the Gospel to a remote tribal group in the mountains of southwest China is a classic story of missionary success.[2] His biography leaves one with a lasting impression regarding his view of the importance of prayer. As he saw the magnitude of the task he felt God calling him to do, he solicited prayer from a small group of believers in England who committed themselves to faithful intercession.

Fraser repeatedly credited God's work among this remote China tribe to the prayer commitment of this small band of English men and women. Fraser's letters frequently reminded them that their prayer to the Omnipresent God was just as effective as was his prayer and work while he was in the villages.

God may call any one of us to a prayer ministry that will have as much effect on the eventual outcome of an effort as that of any person

---

[2] *Mountain Rain* by Eileen Fraser Crossman, or *Behind the Ranges* by Geraldine Taylor.

directly involved in the work.

•

You must avoid unrealistic expectations regarding faith in ministry. Our tendency is to see Elijah's faith only in what took place on Mount Carmel when he called fire from heaven and prayed for rain to bring an end to the drought. We fail to see this same Elijah in hiding for three years, sitting by a brook and watching it run dry, taking cover in a foreign city to escape detection, and finally fleeing from Jezebel who had sworn to kill him by the following day (1 Kings 17-19).

Hebrews 11:32-34 tells us that faith will not always be immediately rewarded. Unnamed men and women who lived by faith were tortured, jeered, flogged, imprisoned, stoned and left destitute. History also reminds us that many who are remembered today for their courageous faith in proclaiming the Gospel or translating Scripture into the common language of their day never saw the results in their own lifetimes.

Undertaking a ministry in faith does not presume that you will see immediate results or even its eventual completion. We must never attempt to measure our faith by the success of a ministry.

•

We want to "bear much fruit" in ministry for Jesus' sake. John 12:24 gives Jesus' instruction for that effectiveness:

"Truly, truly, I say to you, unless a grain of wheat falls into the earth and dies, it remains by itself alone; but if it dies, it bears much fruit." (NASB)

Jesus is telling us that we must die to ourselves if we want to bear fruit. Those of us who live outside of the persecuted Church often understand Jesus' reference to dying as relating to non-material issues such as our personal interests or our self-will. However, that *death* may also pertain to our health, our finances, or any other area of our lives that God wants to use. Two practical questions come from this observation:

1.  Can personal suffering promote ministry?
2.  Does suffering begin only after I express my willingness to submit to adversity if God so chooses?

I related the incident in which I felt God gave me a choice to see Him work either through healing of my diabetes or through greatly expanding an existing ministry. Though I am not entirely certain why, I began praying, "Lord, do anything in my life you want to in order to accomplish that impossible ministry task." I look back four years later and realize how terribly costly that request has been in terms of my health, my finances, my employment, and some other crucial areas as well. Yet, I rejoice in what has been accomplished in both my personal growth in faith and in ministry.

It wasn't until recently, however, that the connection between personal adversity and ministry dawned on me. I often wondered if God really worked in that seemingly ruthless way. In other words, if I would let Him cause me to suffer, in trade He would promote a ministry or something else that was supposedly His will. But God is not trading tit-for-tat. He does not delight in my suffering even though He may purposely bring it into my life. He brings adversity into my life so that I will learn to trust Him more. My faith will grow through trial. That is the answer I was looking for. I will also be able to serve Him more effectively in ministry as my faith grows.

Yes, in one sense, God will increase my effectiveness in a ministry if I allow Him to bring adversity into my life. But it is not because He is exacting a price for His blessing in the ministry. It is because He is nurturing my faith so that He can more effectively work through that faith in accomplishing ministry results of His choosing.

The second question evolves from the first. Does God wait until I express that willingness before He will start the process? Certainly there will be experiences in life when we see God's response only after we have expressed our willingness to be obedient. On the other hand, I have often realized how perfectly God timed events with my health. Thirty-five years ago He began the process that is now resulting in the rather severe complications of diabetes. (In fact, He probably started the process with a childhood disease when I was six that is a precursor to diabetes.) Nonetheless, He has arranged all these events so that the complications have coincided with my willingness to allow Him to do as He wishes.

I could analyze this endlessly. If I was a non-believer, the same sequence of health deterioration may have occurred. All I really need to acknowledge today is that God started a series of events in both my physical and spiritual life so that they complemented each other in spiritual growth and ministry.

———————  •  ———————

# *16* Cursing Fig Trees, Moving Mountains

Matthew 21:18-21 tells of Jesus cursing a fig tree because it had no fruit. The disciples were astonished at how quickly the fig tree withered. Jesus replied:

"I tell you the truth, if you have faith and do not doubt, not only can you do what was done to the fig tree, but also you can say to this mountain, 'Go, throw yourself into the sea,' and it will be done. If you believe, you will receive whatever you ask for in prayer."

Jesus twice used this hyperbole of casting a mountain into the sea. In Matthew 17 He used it as a rebuke for His disciples' *lack* of faith. In Matthew 21, He used it to encourage them to exercise more faith.

When we read these and similar verses, we are confronted with the question, "Are miracles required as a validation of faith?"

•

I don't want to debate whether or not miracles happen today except to note that either of two extremes is inappropriate. One extreme requires that one who has faith be able to educe miraculous manifestations. This goes far beyond the requirements of Scripture. The other extreme denies that God may still use miracles and healing today. This inappropriately limits God. God is free to do whatever He wants when it is consistent with His Holy nature, using whomever He chooses to accomplish it.

•

Are miracles required as a validation of faith? I see nothing in Scripture that leads me to believe that faith is confirmed by the ability to perform a miracle. In fact, in Matthew 7:22-23 Jesus said,

"Many will say to me on that day, 'Lord, Lord, did we not prophesy in your name, and in your name drive out demons and perform many miracles?' Then I will tell them plainly, 'I never knew you. Away from me, you evildoers!'"

The section *Faith and discerning God's will* in Chapter 4 suggests that, as you grow in faith, you will become more dependent upon the *Person* of God and less dependent upon *circumstances as a confirmation* of God's leading. The question we are asking in this chapter has a parallel application. If miracles could confirm my faith, I would then be relying on these manifestations to substantiate my faith rather than on God Himself. This is exactly the opposite response God wants from me. He wants me to trust *Him*, not miracles or my ability to perform them.

On the other hand, this does not say that God cannot choose to heal or perform some other miracle in response to a believer's faith.

•

There is a practical application of faith that you must understand. Another's healing generally results in little direct benefit to the life of the one praying for that healing. On the other hand, when you take *personal* risks in faith, your faith has an immediate impact on your own life.

*The most appropriate way to learn faith is by facing high* **personal** *risk.* Aside from pride associated with the "power" to heal—which is never an appropriate motivation for exercising faith—most miracles or healings require little personal risk. God wants you to grow in areas that concern you. *Relying on God to produce faith in your own life is of greater value in living by faith than seeking faith in order to perform miracles.*

I would be skeptical of anyone claiming to be able to perform miracles by faith who was unable—or unwilling—to deal with difficult personal issues in a manner which demonstrated an implicit trust in God.

•

In 2 Corinthians 12 Paul described the "thorn in his flesh" which God did not take away. In the same way that you cannot discredit either your own or someone else's faith because it is unable to perform miracles, neither can you discredit yourself or another by pointing to a physical or emotional problem God chooses not to remove.

•

Do not evaluate your growth in faith on your ability to perform miracles. Measure your growth in faith by your increasing willingness to let God lead you in the difficult events of daily living and ministry.

———————  •  ———————

# 17 The Tension of Faith

L iving by faith introduces a tension foreign to the normal flow of human life.

God created humanity with a natural inclination to find the simplest, the most understandable, the most predictable, the least costly, and the safest way to accomplish routine tasks in life. This is why we have automatic washing machines rather than scrub boards and automobiles rather than animal-drawn carts. It is also why society has developed many of its institutions. Banks replace buried tin cans as a safe repository of money and courts of law replace vigilantism. This tendency is important to human survival and is entirely appropriate when properly used.

Living by faith often forces the believer into nonconformity with this normal human tendency. Rather than responding in the same way others in society will to an impending crisis, the believer living by faith will feel obligated to seek God's will before taking direct action. To add further uncertainty to the crisis, God may direct the believer to react in a way that does not seem to protect personal interests. Finally, living by faith will require the believer to wait and allow God to respond in His own time.

By its very nature, living by faith is often oriented toward choosing the *most* difficult, the *least* understandable, the *least* predictable, the *most* costly, and the *most* risky way to face the severest crises of life. This is done so that we might learn how to trust God more so that, in turn, we can face even greater difficulty, deal with more unknowns, and face increased personal risk!

•

What has just been said is important. If you are intent on learning to live by faith, a tension will be introduced into your life that is contrary to normal human expectation. You should not be surprised if you begin to grapple with issues you never experienced when you were content with a *comfortable* Christian life. Understand that living by faith will force you to rethink morés (customs or manners) in your society and your personal response to them.

Because that process in your life of faith will be very personal, you will often receive little guidance from either your secular or Christian peers. You will become less able to rely on *standardized* and *socially accepted* behavior. Again, this is an area in which you will face personal risk. You will be charting new directions in your life, and you will be prone to making mistakes.

•

Does this tension in a life of faith give you insight into the extent of sin's influence on human nature? At the very core of our being, we are in rebellion against God. Our human nature compels us to trust ourselves and our society rather than God.

This is also why you—even as a believer—are still incapable of loving or trusting God in your own strength. Your human nature prevents it. It is only when you allow God to do that work in you that you become capable of loving Him, trusting Him, or living a godly life.

•

We can credit God with giving us the natural tendency to simplify and make life more understandable, even though living by faith will supersede that tendency in certain respects. In what is called *common grace*, God has so endowed the human spirit that it can survive in a fallen world.

•

God will not abandon you in this process. It is of the greatest concern to Almighty God that you learn to live by faith. Jesus is the Author and the Perfecter of your faith. If you will trust Him, He will never fail to lead you to a more mature faith in Him. It is never His purpose to frustrate you as you learn to trust Him. However, it is His purpose that you rely less on the conventional means that your society provides and more directly on Him as a Person.

•

If all of these risks and difficulties are certain, why would anyone purposely attempt to live by faith? Certainly not because the life of faith will be one of ease. My own answer is simply this: *I want to learn to trust Jesus because I love Him, and because I love Him, I want to know Him better.* That is why I want to live by faith.

———— • ————

# *18* Issues in Society That Hinder Faith

The thesis of this chapter is not that certain social institutions are inherently corrupt while others are acceptable. The assertion is that *any social institution that a believer uses to replace his or her dependence on God is—for that individual—a functional substitute for God.*[1]

The more familiar biblical term for a *functional substitute for God* is an *idol.* We are quick to see Israel's sin in serving Baal. Yet, we are terribly slow to see our own *idolatry* when we depend on insurance policies, use medicine, make investments, or depend on government agencies because we are unwilling to trust God.

•

Even a cursory evaluation of technological and social development over the past 200 years (approximately the span of time since the beginning of the Industrial Revolution) indicates that humanity is set on taking greater control of the unknown. There is much to be thankful for in progress in education, medicine, transportation, and personal conveniences. Nonetheless, any of these areas can be used either wisely or with unwitting dependency by today's believer.

Four areas requiring the greatest caution are medicine, insurance, financial investments (including pensions), and legal/government institutions. None of these are inherently wrong. On the contrary, each can be used to very worthwhile advantage.

Yet, the believer who wants to depend more on God must carefully scrutinize *all* of these institutions for potential abuse.

---

[1] This paragraph uses two terms that require definition. A *social institution* is a significant practice, relationship, or organization in a society. The term can be used of a country's legal system, the practice of medicine, religion in a broad sense (or a specific organized church in a restricted sense), the provision and use of insurance to protect real property or intangible assets, and so on. A *functional substitute* was defined earlier as an institution that replaces another primary institution when that primary institution becomes inaccessible or unresponsive, or is held in low esteem. This chapter adds the specific qualifier *for God* to the more general term *functional substitute.* In the context of this chapter, *a functional substitute for God* identifies a social institution that is used to replace God as the One who provides.

•

We can never say that God will *always* lead a believer to do one thing, or *never* to do another. Nonetheless, a believer's use of some social institutions may be a prudent use of the resources God has given. Use of other social institutions by the same believer may indicate lack of reliance on God's provision or sovereignty.

There would be little debate that someone with a broken arm should go to a doctor, or that homeowner's insurance should be carried on the family home, or that a pension is a wise part of retirement planning. On the other hand, for the believer intent on living by faith, we may question such things as using genetic screening followed by radical surgeries as a protection against potential health problems, buying high-dollar trip life insurance at the airport, using fertility drugs, or initiating lawsuits for defamation of character.

In each case, believers wanting to live by faith need to determine the place of their trust relative to the sovereignty of God. There will be times when prudently making use of our society's institutions does not represent any lack of trust in God. It may be as simple as determining that it is easier to budget for a quarterly insurance payment which includes collision coverage than it would be to use savings to repair an automobile damaged in an accident.

At other times the same believer may have a clear sense that seeking medical treatment, buying insurance, placing undue emphasis on financial security in retirement, or depending on government agencies is contrary to trusting God.

•

Those attempting to live by faith will have difficulty in this area because the majority of American Christians unwittingly accept many *functional substitutes for God*. There has been such a proliferation of technologies and social services since World War II that it is often difficult to identify the number of resources we have today which have removed us from direct dependence on God. In that same interval of time, the Western social conscience has radically shifted—not only to accommodate technology—but also to accept it as the *norm*. In the early 1900s, certain medical emergencies could only be left to *Providence*. If the patient lived, there was gratitude. If the patient died, it was "God's will." Today, we are increasingly faced with medical ethical debates as to the appropriate time to remove life support and so on. Much of this debate is fueled by the developing social consciousness which demands that every patient must be given—and avail themselves of—the highest level of medical technology in order to prolong life. (Interestingly, this increasing demand is concurrent with the debate regarding assisted suicide. Both discussions grow out of the human desire to assume more control of life.)

Medical ethicists are well ahead of most believers in many of these issues. The medical ethicist may realize that there is need for caution. Yet, the believer may give little consideration to trusting God with an outcome while continuing to use every avenue of medical help available. The modern Church has generally accepted all of these functional substitutes for God as being routine and acceptable rather than emphasizing the need to exercise faith when making individual decisions.

•

These are areas in which you must be extremely careful. Do not assume that if you want to live by faith you must refuse all help that does not come directly from God. At the same time, you must be discerning so that you do not fail to recognize when you would be using functional substitutes rather than depending on God Himself.

•

Irrespective of the desire to trust God, a believer cannot ignore society's valid need to create equitable living conditions for the majority. For good reasons, you can no longer put a child who is not wearing a lifejacket in a private boat, claiming to trust in God for the child's protection. The Coast Guard mandates that the child wear a lifejacket. For the well-being of others, you cannot refuse to buy property insurance, choosing instead to trust God to protect your new home against fire. Your mortgage company will not finance the house unless you carry homeowner's insurance. Because the financial future of others sharing Social Security is at stake, you cannot refuse to pay your share of retirement withholding tax.

I do not think that the believer must react to these regulations and laws as though our freedoms are being challenged. They are designed for the greater good of society. It is not our prerogative to pass the risk of our personal faith on to others. We cannot ask the mortgage company—or a neighbor whose house would also be jeopardized—to carry the risk of our trust in God. We cannot ask others to support us in our old age because we want to avoid paying Social Security tax.

•

Nonetheless, you will often be alone as you make decisions to trust God rather than the functional substitutes provided by society. You must fully realize that there are multiple reasons why certain institutions operate as they do. For example, doctors and medical staff—as well as the insurance industries funding your treatment—have established procedures that work best, on average, for everyone concerned. They are reticent to take either the time or the risk to treat your condition differently. You must also realize that in our free enterprise economy, your medical treatment is a source of revenue for the medical and insurance institutions.

You will not find it either easy or stress-free to make a decision regarding your medical treatment when you are placing the emphasis on trusting God rather than medicine. Dealing with the medical community and insurance carriers can be difficult—if not costly—when you decline prescribed treatment.

•

Let me anticipate two areas of question you will face. The first question might be, "Must I choose either to accept *all* medical treatment recommended or to decline *everything*?" The second question could be, "Can I change my mind later?"

Most experiences involving faith are dynamic rather than static. That means that *progressive* decisions will be made as the situation unfolds. In few areas of life will you make a single decision at the beginning that will determine the entire outcome. I don't see why it would be any different for medical treatment or other areas of living by faith. As you carefully consider before God what you are doing, you may add insurance later, or you may stop taking a medication during the course of treatment. You may elect certain treatment but forego other procedures.

•

The broader issue of making financial investment for the purpose of retirement is likely one of the most difficult issues a believer will face when living by faith. Medicine and property insurance issues are often more immediate. However, retirement investment is difficult because future needs are unknown.

Inflation, declining personal health, loss of a spouse, increasing cost of retirement housing or assisted living, leisure activities during retirement, and many other issues make retirement investment one of society's highest priorities.

You will need to evaluate this area carefully. The typical Christian response is to assume that a full retirement package from employment and investments is God's way of caring for His children. The Christian community is reticent to reevaluate that premise by applying Scriptural passages such as Matthew 6 to our future financial planning.

●

If your goal is to live by faith, at some point you must ask God for direction regarding your investments (or pension) and your willingness to trust Him to provide for you during your retirement years. *This does not presume that you must forego pension or insurance benefits.* It simply means that you must allow God to direct your decisions.

This is not a place to act foolishly or in response to others' suggestions. Yet, retirement programs may be—for many believers —one of our most deeply entrenched functional substitutes for God.

●

Believers have become increasingly dependent on government provisions for their personal well-being. Government-sponsored retirement programs, health care, and housing tax benefits affect almost *all* believers in this country. Others may also use government financed housing loans, education loans or grants, housing programs, unemployment or disability benefits, welfare assistance, and so on. Many believers own or work for businesses that are dependent on government subsidy.

In recent years, the Church has become involved in state and federal politics because believers have become so largely dependent on government finances.

Society has become increasingly litigious. Civil courts are routinely used for personal gain. Believers have not been immune to this abuse.

A believer living by faith must very carefully evaluate personal dependence and use of our legal/governmental institutions.

●

The four institutional categories of medicine, insurance, investment (or pension), and legal/government intervention are by no means a comprehensive list. Our society is rife with social institutions that become functional substitutes for God. If you want to live by faith, you will need to evaluate everything in your life that has the potential for replacing your trust in God.

———— ● ————

# *19* Issues in Church Life That Hinder Faith

S ecular society is not the only place where your faith will be tested. The evangelical Church may also inadvertently hinder your life of faith.

•

An important hindrance to faith comes because the evangelical Church lacks awareness of our secular world's use of functional substitutes for God. (This is true irrespective of how functional substitutes for God may be identified.)

The Church rarely overtly promotes society's functional substitutes for God. In fact, the evangelical Church seldom has any comment on the subject, which is precisely the problem. Just as the Temple worshipper in the Old Testament should have been concerned by Israel's idol worship, so the evangelical Christian today should be concerned by the encroachment of society's functional substitutes for God on the Church. In reality, the problem is basically ignored.

It is impossible for the Christian Church to endorse the antithesis of faith while simultaneously trying to encourage believers to live by faith.

•

Ignorance of functional substitutes for God is an important reason why a believer wanting to live by faith will encounter apathy from Christian peers. It would genuinely surprise the average church member if a fellow believer were to question unrestricted use of medicine, insurance, investments, or dependence on legal and government institutions. Rather than finding the average church to be an institution which promotes living by faith, the believer wanting to live by faith will realize that he or she is part of a small minority who desire to trust God rather than society's institutions.

•

Within the Church today, one will hear reasoning that masks the need of allowing God to lead the believer through faith. The logic sounds good on the surface because it contains some truth. These half-truths include statements such as, "The believer must make reasonable financial provision for his family," or "Because our body is God's temple, health is an important priority for the believer," or

"God does not call us to be foolish or unprepared," and so on.

Members of the early Church did *not* place an emphasis on protecting personal health when they took mortal risks for the sake of the Gospel. The early Disciples did *not* secure permanent jobs for the purpose of providing for their families. First century believers often took extreme risks in order to preach Christ.

The early Church placed a high priority on living and serving by faith.

•

*In all probability, the evangelical Church hinders a believer's life of faith most because it does not provide role models who live by faith.*

Theological training does not produce faith. Only a life of trusting God will produce a faith that can be modeled for others.

When a church leader is growing in faith, the result will be an effective personal ministry as well as an example that others can emulate.

There will, of course, be those who do not wish to forego their *comfortable* Christianity. When a church leader is actively modeling a life of faith, there will be those who will be strongly attracted to this vibrant Christianity, but there will also be some who will object and ultimately leave the congregation.

•

If you are not in a primary position of leadership in your own congregation, you will find that pursuing faith will be even more difficult. In almost any congregation the presumption is that the paid staff members are the *most spiritual.* It would seem inconceivable that a lay person in the congregation would have more awareness of living by faith than the staff personnel. (This will not be true if the church's leaders are themselves growing in faith.)

•

Please do not misunderstand what I just said about the church and its leadership. Most evangelical churches would express no overt opposition to living by faith. In fact, I could imagine that faith experiences would be referred to from the pulpit, would be the object of "praise" mention in the church prayer bulletin, and would be discussed in adult Sunday School classes.

But I would also expect to see it dismissed (albeit politely) as being *your* unique experience in the Christian life. It would be viewed as something between you and God with no expectation that it has relevance for anyone else. You would be congratulated, and then the issue of living by faith would again be forgotten. Should you mention other faith experiences, you would soon have the feeling that you were saying too much or that others felt you were attempting to draw attention to yourself.

I have, of course, overstated my case. Sadly, however, I think there is an element of truth to what I have said.

•

You may often feel alone as you learn to live by faith. Certainly, there will be times when you will need to make decisions contrary to the recommendations of those in the medical community or service industries. At the same time, you may also find yourself unsupported by your fellow believers. You may even find that your desire to trust God will become a cause of alienation.

You will need to be wise in your evaluation of this situation. If the misunderstanding comes because you lack tact or are strident in expressing your views, then it is your responsibility to make corrections. On the other hand, if you have been prudent as you pursue faith, you can almost be certain that relations with some believers will cool because of their desire to maintain the status quo.

In this latter case, quietly pursue faith in your own life. Do not take this as an opportunity to hold others publicly accountable for what you presume to be a lack of faith.

———————————◆———————————

## FOR PASTORS ONLY

I understand some of the difficulties that you as a pastor face. Your job is difficult because you must be the role model and the administrator for so many different people in the congregation. Nonetheless, you are accountable before God to prepare these people to meet Jesus.

Think of 10 people from your congregation who have shown the greatest growth during your tenure as their pastor. Now, try to visualize their responses when they first stand before Jesus in Heaven. How do you think they might report their life? Will they recount a life that evidenced biblical priorities, including an effective life of faith? Or will they falter in an attempt to explain their involvement with church programs and numerous religious activities? *How well are you preparing them for that first meeting with Jesus?*

May I be candid in my next observation without being judgmental? *I believe I see pastors frequently trying to encourage people to grow in Christ without themselves having a clear idea of what that growth should be.* I hear sermons dealing with theology, with exegetical studies, with ethical and moral issues, and with correctives for human needs and injustices. But I seldom hear men who can say with credibility, "I have learned to love Jesus, and I have learned to live by faith; now from Scripture, let me show you how you, too, can deeply love Jesus and live by faith."

Simply stated, *a pastor cannot lead his people into a walk with Jesus that he himself has not experienced.*

I trust that it has been clear throughout this book that I have no secret "formula" for living by faith. God leads each individual in living by faith as He chooses. *I still must ask if you are living by faith? Have you learned what it means to trust Jesus in a way that pleases God? As a result, are you now able to model and teach that same information to members of your congregation?*

Let me give more detail to the story of George and Mary Müller.[1] In 1830 at the age of 25, Müller had been the co-pastor of two congregations for several years. Both congregations were showing considerable growth. During that time he concluded that the common practice of pew rent was a violation of James 2:1-6 which forbids preferential treatment of the rich. The rental price for pews at the front of the church was higher than for pews in the back of the church. The fact that his salary as pastor came from the pew rents made this issue personally significant.

Shortly after their marriage in 1830, George and Mary Müller decided that they would no longer accept a fixed salary, but would depend solely on God for their financial well-being. Müller then announced that pews in the church would no longer be rented. Instead, a box was placed at the back of the church for voluntary offerings for the support of the pastors. The Müllers decided from that time on that they would never mention financial need to others, neither for themselves, nor for any ministry they undertook. They took the need to God alone in prayer. (During his lifetime, the Müllers gave almost

---

[1] This information comes from the book *George Müller, Delighted in God!* by Roger Steer, Harold Shaw Publishers, 1981.

£1,500,000 [$5,683,000 in 1997 U.S. dollars] to many different ministry needs.2 *Not once in that entire time was there either a public or private appeal for funds. The printed annual reports never solicited funds. Prayer was their only avenue of request.*)

For about six years the Müllers' faith grew as they depended on God for everything in their temporal lives. Then they began searching for a way to teach the people in their congregations how to live by faith. In 1836, George and Mary Müller started an orphanage for the *primary* purpose of demonstrating to others that God was able through prayer alone to provide everything necessary for their orphanage work. *The Müllers had already learned many valuable personal lessons in living by faith. Now they wanted to show others how they, too, could live by faith.* The primary purpose of the Müllers' orphanages was to model faith in a God who was able to provide through prayer alone.

Does your faith please God? Is it a faith you can *model* for believers in your own congregation?

----------------------------------- • -----------------------------------

2 Expressing the purchasing power of the British pound during Müller's lifetime in today's United States' dollar has numerous complications. Nonetheless, if we do not assign some dollar value, the significance of the Müllers' giving would largely be lost.

We have arbitrarily selected 1860 as the exchange rate date. (The Müllers started supporting ministry solely through prayer in 1835, and George died in 1898.) The most conservative exchange rate information lists £1.00 as being equal to $4.60 in 1860. The U.S. dollar value decreased from $1.00 in 1860 to $17.43 in 1997. Using this single 1997 value for the dollar, in their lifetime the Müllers gave approximately $5,683,000 in U.S. dollars. Only £1,000,000 ($3,790,000) actually went to orphanage work. In addition, the Müllers supported literature work, schools, and missions. For a period of time, they were almost the sole supporters of the *entire* China Inland Mission work under Hudson Taylor. At one point Müllers were *personally supporting* almost 200 foreign missionaries at approximately £10,000 ($379,000) a year.

However, if we use exchange rates that are adjusted for all inflation and cost of living increases we obtain considerably larger figures because the British Pound decreased sharply in value between 1910 and present. In their lifetime, the Müllers directed £1,453,513 13s 3d to ministry. According to **www.ex.ac.uk/~RDavies/arian/current/howmuch.html** £1,454,000 in 1860 equaled £66,549,000 in 2000, and the exchange rate was £1 for $1.61 (US) on January 1 of 2000. Using these conversion rates, the Müllers raised $107,143,000 for ministry. At this exchange rate, the £1,000,000 given to the orphanage work becomes $73,690,000.

# *20* Pitfalls in Living by Faith

As you learn to live by faith, you will need to identify and avoid a number of hazards. This chapter describes only a few of these potential problem areas.

•

You will discover very early that living by faith does not necessarily result in quick answers to prayer. It is God's prerogative to decide when He will grant your requests. You must *never* gauge your growth in faith by measuring the time interval between your requests and God's answers.

•

You must learn to distinguish between *faith* and *unwise expectations*. God may lead you to pray intently for something which appears to be humanly impossible. Throughout both Scripture and history there are examples of this kind of prayer. For example, even though there had been severe drought for three years, according to 1 Kings 18, Elijah prayed specifically for rain and God miraculously sent torrential rain on the same day.

At the same time, you must exercise both caution and wisdom as you live by faith. Without compromising your willingness to take risks in faith, you must learn to pray for those things which please God and accomplish His purpose.

•

Always remember that *learning to trust God is the purpose of your life of faith*. The primary purpose is *not* so that you can work miracles or use displays of amazing supernatural power as a means of revealing God to others.

•

You must exercise special caution as you learn to live by faith. All religious people—including the most well-intentioned Christians—share the propensity for self-deception. Because you want your faith to produce results, you will be inclined to look for any sign indicating that God answered your prayer. You will need to be careful that you do not let your mind arrange details so that mere random events are distorted to appear as answers to your faith.

We must be careful to allow God to act in our lives without falling into the trap of self-deception. Nothing is gained by wanting so much for faith to work that we unconsciously fabricate an outcome that we then claim as God's response.

I find it equally offensive to see others being manipulated by the vocal intonation of the one praying, with touching and contrived behavior, or by control of the environment with music or lighting so that what follows appears to be a miraculous manifestation. We must constantly be aware that we neither attempt to manipulate others—or allow ourselves to be manipulated—in our desire to live by faith.

●

One of the great joys of learning to live by faith is the awareness of a viable and growing faith. However, this awareness of personal growth never allows for arrogance or pride.

●

As you learn to live by faith, you must be careful that you do not presume to "know everything about faith."

Nonetheless, it is appropriate to be discerning of others' expressions of faith and cautiously evaluate them for biblical accuracy. Your discernment may keep both you and others from error. At the same time, you must generously make allowance for God's leading in their lives even though it differs from how He has led you in the past.

●

You must avoid complacency in faith. There may have been difficult early lessons that you now feel competent to handle. Your tendency will be to stay in the comfort zone of the lessons already learned. In order to continue growing in faith, you must be willing to let God lead you into new areas of uncertainty. He will not always meet your future needs in the same ways He met past needs. He will continue to force you to trust *Him* rather than relying on the skills you have acquired from the past.

●

You must always remember that you will continue your life of faith in the same way you started. Your faith is a result of God's gracious provision in your life. Just as you were completely dependent on God to give you faith as you began your life of faith, so you will continue to be dependent on God to provide ongoing faith in the future.

———————  ●  ———————

# 21 Spiritual Warfare

Complacent Christians probably present little threat to Satan. It is when you begin living by faith that he will vent his fury on you. It should be obvious that Satan fears the believer who is living by faith because faith is the avenue through which God works.

•

Be certain of the truth of these three passages as you begin your life of faith:

Be self-controlled and alert. Your enemy the devil prowls around like a roaring lion looking for someone to devour. Resist him, standing firm in the faith (I Peter 5:8-9).

"When [the Devil] lies, he speaks his native language, for he is a liar and the father of lies" (John 8:44).

But encourage one another daily...so that none of you may be hardened by sin's deceitfulness (Hebrews 3:13).

If you are living by faith, you are constantly under Satan's surveillance. He wants to destroy you. You are now in intense spiritual warfare, though you always have God's protection.

Satan's primary tactic is deception. He is the "father of lies." He is the Deceiver. He can show a marked degree of success among complacent evangelical Christians because they have been deceived into believing that *comfortable* and *safe* Christianity is the norm. Satan has also convinced many that religious behavior and organizational church activity is the epitome of the Christian life. This notion—with its accompanying activity—takes the believer's attention away from an intimate faith in Almighty God.

But if you are pursuing faith, you are going to break free of Satan's bondage of *complacency*. So what defense will he use now?

True to his character, he will use every means at his disposal to *deceive* you. Think about *deception* and how it can defeat your life of faith.

SELF DOUBT: "I don't have enough strength to live by faith." "I am only a layman. I have no special training." "This isn't how other Christians live. Why should I think *I* am right?"

FAILURE AND SIN: "I have honestly tried to live by faith before but I just couldn't succeed." "God remembers that specific sin; He just couldn't accept my faltering faith now."

PRESENT LIMITATIONS: "I need to provide for my family. I don't have time (or can't afford) to live by faith." "My family wouldn't be supportive; I don't have a place to pray privately."

DOUBT AFTER BEGINNING: "I think I started okay, but then I committed a terrible sin. I just can't continue." "I am trying to live by faith, but nothing is happening." "I thought God was leading me to ask for something important, but He didn't answer." "My prayer life is too ordinary. I expected it to become intense."

•

Satan's primary deception is to focus your attention on *your* ability. Of course you can't live by faith. But you are not the Author and Perfecter of your faith. Jesus is. Can Jesus strengthen you so that you can live by faith? He most certainly can!

Let me give you a reminder that I personally use when I face doubts or uncertainty regarding my faith:

1. Does Jesus have the *power* to complete this task? Yes, He does because He had enough power to create the entire Universe.

2. Does Jesus care enough for me *personally* to complete this task? Yes, He cares for me enough that He paid a terrible price for my Salvation. Because of that, He must also care for everything else in my life in order to protect His investment.

3. Does Jesus have the *time* to become involved in this task? Yes, He is Infinite (Absolute). Though this task will require His attention and effort, it will in no way deplete His resources.

4. Does Jesus *want* to do what I am asking? Of these four questions, this is the only question that might possibly be answered "no." This last question must be answered after carefully considering Scripture and the Spirit's leading.

•

*Anything Satan would do to convince you that you cannot live by faith is his classic technique of deception.* Jesus has the *power* to give you faith. Jesus *cares for you enough* to give you all of the *time* and *help* necessary to enable you to live by faith. Finally, Scripture is abundantly clear that Jesus *wants* you to live by faith. Therefore, nothing but your *unwillingness* to let Jesus produce faith in you will prevent you from living by faith.

•

When we consider spiritual warfare, we usually think of direct confrontation with antagonists of the Gospel. When we read the book of Acts, we certainly see this conflict between believers and their enemies. Paul and others were flogged, heckled, stoned, and rejected by those resisting the Gospel. However, what was Satan attempting to do when Paul was imprisoned for two years in Caesarea, followed by two more years of house arrest in Rome? With the exception of the trip between Caesarea and Rome, Paul was probably safer and more free of physical trauma during his incarceration than at any time during his active preaching. Though we can only surmise, it was probably the *monotonous routine* of prison life that Satan was attempting to use to reduce Paul to ineffectiveness. Instead, Paul wrote his four Prison Epistles!

•

There may be times when you will face clear opposition to your life of faith from antagonists to the Gospel. These will be times when you can identify your involvement in spiritual warfare.

There will be another form of spiritual warfare which will catch you by surprise if you are not prepared for it. True to his character, the Deceiver distorts even spiritual warfare. He wants to defeat you, but he knows that if the battle *looks* like spiritual warfare, you will be more dependent on God. So his solution may be to disguise spiritual warfare as *temporal* concerns. If he can defeat you through financial, health, family, or professional concerns, he can still keep you from an effective life of faith. But he will be able to do so without arousing your awareness that it is spiritual warfare and that you need God to deliver you.

•

By no means is all human hardship the result of spiritual warfare. Even if you are not living by faith, calamity will come as a result of the general condition of mankind. On the other hand, if you are living by faith, you must carefully evaluate your life and determine—if possible—if you are a special target of Satan's attacks.

If you are living by faith, it is likely that Satan will use as many hardships in your temporal life as possible in order to defeat you. Be prepared!

Be cautious, however. Do not blame everything on Satan. Remember what was also said in Chapter 11 (*Faith and Adversity*) about God's use of adversity as a tool to promote your growth in faith.

# *22* Avoiding Self-Immolation

To *immolate* is defined as *to offer in sacrifice.* In this chapter, *self-immolation* means an intentional act of self-destruction.

Several themes have recurred throughout this book that may seem to imply self-immolation. This includes the emphasis on *risk* as an inherent part of faith and *adversity* as a means of growth.

•

Under normal circumstances, there is no need for the believer to seek adversity. It is pointless and foolish to make life any more difficult than it already is. We certainly expect that life will be harsh at times. But that does not need to be by our own doing.

•

However, the above statement is not a binding principle. Remember the description in Chapter 9 of Paul and Silas willingly receiving a flogging at Philippi. Though we are given no reason why they willingly submitted to the treatment, we can assume that they knew that they would be hurt. Nonetheless, they chose to receive the flogging because it better served the cause of the Gospel.

•

It is clear when reading either historical accounts of the suffering Church—*Foxe's Book of Martyrs,* for example—or recent accounts of the suffering Church in China and other repressed countries, that these believers could have avoided persecution had they been willing to compromise. In effect, they chose to suffer.

•

It is interesting to note the fuller meaning in Jesus' words to His Disciples:

"And you will be my *witnesses* in Jerusalem, and in all Judea and Samaria, and to the ends of the earth" (Acts 1:8). (Emphasis added.)

The English word *witnesses* comes from the Greek word *martyros* from which we get our English word *martyr.* The word meant *to be a witness unto death.* The word did not indicate to the Greek-speaking listener that he or she *would* die for their faith, but it meant that their testimony was not to change at any time, even if it cost them their life.

In Acts 9, Saul (Paul) was confronted by Jesus and subsequently acknowledged Him as Messiah. While the blinded Saul was praying in Damascus, Jesus appeared to Ananias and told him to go and lay his hands on Saul in order to restore his sight. Then Jesus made an interesting comment to Ananias in Acts 9:16:

"I will show him how much he must suffer for my name."

Saul received an interesting introduction to the Christian life. Jesus did not mince words. He told Saul *how much* he would suffer. When we read descriptions of Paul's suffering in Acts and the Epistles, we can only imagine the details he was given!

•

Peter told the suffering Church:

Dear friends, do not be surprised at the painful trial you are suffering, as though something strange were happening to you. But rejoice that you participate in the sufferings of Christ, so that you may be overjoyed when his glory is revealed...If you suffer as a Christian, do not be ashamed, but praise God that you bear that name (1 Peter 4:12-13, 16).

•

We must realize that suffering is a part of living by faith. This does not mean that all Christians will suffer equally, or that suffering will be in the form of physical persecution. But it means that any *may* suffer if they are unwilling to compromise their faith.

At the same time, unless God leads otherwise, there is no need to make life any more difficult than necessary by seeking adversity.

Nothing in this book should be understood to mean that you must attempt to suffer in order to live by faith.

————————  •  ————————

# *23* Course Correction

What can you do if you have spent a lifetime in church and religious activities, but you now realize that you have never truly lived by faith?

The answer is encouraging. You can *still* pursue faith, regardless of your age.

•

Before I suggest some corrective measures for those making a late start in living a life of real faith, I want to restate three principles:

1. You must understand that living by faith is not an option. God *expects* you to live by faith. You cannot please Him *without* faith.

2. You must avoid minimizing the importance of living by faith. Church members are often placated with the assurance that all believers are living by faith. Yes, if you are truly a child of God, you have received salvation through faith. But salvation alone does not mean that your daily life is an ongoing life of faith.

   *If you cannot currently point to instances in your life of trusting God, you are not living by faith.* Many adults in our evangelical churches regularly attend Sunday School and church services and are "busy" in church activities. They listen to Christian radio and follow various Bible studies. They may even read their Bibles and pray daily. In-and of itself, none of this is living by faith. If this describes your life, then according to Hebrews 11:6, you are not pleasing God. You are merely living a religious life.

   You are living by faith when you trust God rather than relying on conventional means for something you need, or you trust Him for something when that trust incurs otherwise avoidable personal risk. You are also living by faith when you are resting in Him during times of turmoil in your life. If you cannot see these elements of faith in your life, you are not living by faith.

3. On the other hand, you must allow God to lead you individually without trying to copy others' experiences of faith. You will know if you are trusting God for specific concerns in your life. It is an active process of which you will be aware.

•

If you cannot look at your life and clearly see *acting* or *trusting* faith, then I hope that you will take remedial action.

However, I am not suggesting that you "busy" yourself with more religious activities. Your emphasis must be on trusting God rather than spending more time serving your church or other Christian organizations.

•

If you have not been living by faith, then you need to repent—meaning that you need to "turn around and go the opposite direction" (which is the meaning of *repent*). After sin is confessed, however, you are able to start over fresh.

**If we confess our sins, he is faithful and just and will forgive us our sins and purify us from all unrighteousness (1 John 1:9).**

Now, thank God for delivering you from *"all unrighteousness"* and joyfully pursue faith. Your past failures are behind you.

•

As you begin to pursue faith, ask God for two things. First, ask God to give you a deep love for Jesus. Then ask Him to give you faith.

In your own strength, you can neither love Jesus nor trust Him. You must ask Him to give you the capacity to do both. (Carefully review Chapter 5.)

You must also seriously consider the cost of faith. *You will need to give Jesus permission to do anything in your life He chooses that will cause you to trust Him more.* You must also re-orient your response to adversity. Now, rather than immediately asking others' prayer for relief, you will first need to evaluate the lessons God wants you to learn though the adversity. This does not preclude God's eventual deliverance from the trial, but it means that the adversity now has purpose. You cannot run from hardship. You must allow God to use it in your life as He intends.

•

Begin the process of regularly asking God for the faith (and love for Jesus) that He wants you to have for each day. Live in the victory that He will graciously provide faith to you.

God is both sovereign and merciful. Even though you may now deeply regret your late start, trust Him to lead you into whatever faith experiences He has for you. Starting now, He will give you as much faith as He wants you to have for each day. When you stand before Him in Heaven, both you and He will be satisfied with your level of faith. He will not demand more from you then than He is willing to give you now if you become fully obedient in pursuing faith.

For [Yahweh] God is a sun and shield; [Yahweh] bestows favor and honor; *no good thing does he withhold from those whose walk is blameless* (Psalms 84:11). (Emphasis added.)

•

Whether you are a student, an apprentice or young professional, a middle-aged working adult, or a retiree, God is calling you to please Him as you live by faith.

Accept Jesus' offer to be the Author and Perfecter of your faith. Then anticipate your joy in Heaven when you can stand before Him without shame, knowing that your life fulfilled the purpose of His costly sacrifice for you.

———————— • ————————

# Appendix: **The Person of God**

Living by faith is not a human-centered religious experience. In the biblical sense, one living by faith is trusting God (Jesus) for every eventuality in personal life and ministry. Who we understand God to be will directly determine the degree of trust we are willing to place in Him.

Before Jesus' incarnation, Jewish theologians thought they had a reasonable understanding of Yahweh. He was One, Indivisible God. All devout Jews repeated the *sh'ma* during the morning and evening prayer:

Hear O Israel, the Lord our God, the Lord is One.

Then, Jesus claimed to be the I AM. It was for that supposedly blasphemous claim that the Jews picked up stones to kill him.[1]

Jesus had already introduced the *Father* in His teaching. It comes as a surprise to most Christians today that identification of the *Father* was strictly a New Testament concept. The King James Old Testament only capitalizes the word *Father* once when referring to deity (Isaiah 9:6), and that verse refers to Jesus. (The NIV translation capitalizes the word *Father* nine times in the Old Testament. [Deut. 32:6, Ps. 2:7, Ps. 89:26, Isa. 9:6, Isa. 63:16, Isa. 64:8, Jer. 3:4, Jer. 3:19, and Mal. 2:10]. Isaiah 9:6 identifies *Messiah* in reference to Jesus. The other eight verses refer to *Yahweh* rather than the *Father* in the New Testament sense.) The Jews of Jesus' day did not have a concept of *Father*. They thought in terms of a unified God whom they knew as Yahweh.

Jesus introduced the concept of the *Father* being a Person. In itself, that did not challenge the Jewish understanding of a God of Unity. However, when Jesus claimed to also be I AM, He identified both Himself and the Father as God. This clashed with the Jewish understanding of the Unity of God.

---

[1] John 8:48-59 is rich in meaning. Jesus' detractors challenged His statement that "Abraham rejoiced to see My day." Jesus' answer was, "Before Abraham was born, I AM." Nothing could have been a more clear statement of Jesus' intentional identification with Yahweh of the Old Testament. (In Exodus 3:13-15, Moses asked Who was speaking to him from the burning bush. God answered that I AM was speaking.) The Jews then accused Jesus of blaspheming the name of Yahweh and tried to stone Him.

## Graphic representations of God

The purpose of this appendix is to show graphic representations of God without lengthy explanations. This may help you develop a mental picture of the Person of God. As used in this appendix, the term *Person* identifies *individuality* or *being* rather than *humanity*.

Each graphic depiction will be flawed in some way or at least incomplete. Nonetheless, use these mental images of God as you study Scripture. Attempt, with the Spirit's enlightenment, to develop an understanding of God that is biblically accurate and goes beyond the excuse that "God is just too hard to understand. We must simply accept that He is Three but He is also One."

These graphic representations are limited. They merely represent my personal understanding of the Godhead and the inter-relationship of the Father, Jesus, and the Spirit.

## The God of the Old Testament

Figure 1 represents God as He was understood by the Old Testament saints. They understood Him to be Unity. With the exception of special revelation to specific individuals—if, in fact, David understood the Spirit to be a Person—the devout Old Testament Jew understood Yahweh to be a single Person. That was the religious setting of Jesus' day.

## Figure 1

## The New Testament concept of God

Figure 2 represents my understanding of the Godhead as described in the New Testament.

This representation properly shows both the Unity of God and the three Persons of God without contradicting the Absolute nature of Jesus or the Spirit. However, when using this representation, a satisfactory explanation is required for Jesus' statements that He was "under" the Father (see Chapter 8).

1. The concept of the Unity of God is as true in the New Testament as it was in the Old Testament. God did not change His character. However, after Pentecost, Jesus' disciples most certainly understood that Jesus was Messiah. They understood Jesus' title *Emmanuel* to describe exactly His nature as *God with us* (Matt. 1:23). In addition,

**Figure 2**

Jesus had introduced the Spirit as a *Person* rather than a *Force*. In John 15:26 the Spirit is specifically identified as *He* with personality and male gender.

2. Any graphic representation of God must show individual Persons while maintaining the Unity of God. This is indicated with the dashed lines in Figure 2.

3. The Unity of God cannot be compromised. In this figure, He can still be characterized as "God is One."

4. However, according to Jesus' life and teaching, we must recognize that there are three unique Persons within that Unity.

5. There cannot be any designation of *greater* and *lesser* rank among the Persons. If one is Eternal, all are Eternal. If one is Absolute, they must all be Absolute, and so on. (Note the arrow on the left side of the drawing. You can mentally rotate this figure so that any one of the three names may be placed at the top of the drawing. The Father cannot be placed at the apex of a triangle representing the Godhead.)

6. It is this Unity that makes God One. He is One in essential nature. For example, God is Absolute. The Father is Absolute. Jesus is Absolute. So too, the Spirit is Absolute. No other being is Absolute. Therefore, only the Father, Jesus, and the Spirit share this quality of being Absolute. That same quality of uniqueness (Oneness) could be extended to many other areas of their individual and collective attributes.

7. Their unique nature is not the result of a random process of elimination that left only these three with these qualities. They are not identified only by their attributes. They are equally identified by their Unity.

8. The Unity would be destroyed if any one of the three Persons were absent. God does not consist solely of the Father. God is the three Persons in Unity.

The three Persons are recognized as such, and throughout the New Testament are seen to have different functions and relationships to believers. To mention just three, Jesus saves, the Father provides, and the Spirit convicts. Yet, they are in perfect agreement in all of their individual acts.

The terms *God* and *Father* are not synonyms, even though the

Father is fully God. The same is also true of both Jesus and the Spirit. Jesus (or the Spirit) is fully God. Nonetheless, we would not use the terms *God* and *Jesus* as synonyms. Much confusion results from using *God* and *Father* interchangeably. The term *God* should be used to identify the corporate Godhead. The name *Father* is used to identify one Person of the Godhead. However, the term *God the Father* properly identifies the Father.

When Thomas exclaimed "My Lord and my God." he was not identifying Jesus as the Father. He was acknowledging Jesus' nature as God. The idea that "Jesus was his own Father" cannot exist in this explanation as it can within Modalism. (See Figure 5 below.)

Scripture never identifies God as "They." We can speak of the individual Persons of the Godhead, but we can never go beyond the convention of Scripture and speak of God corporately as *They*. (The English language will force us to use *They* or *Their* when describing individual Persons of the Godhead. Nonetheless, we will never use *They* or *Their* of the corporate Godhead.) God is more than merely three equal and Absolute Persons. When speaking of the Persons collectively, Scripture recognizes only the singular form of address or identification.[2] Scripture uses only *Him*, *He* and *His* when speaking of God.

A brief comment needs to be made regarding the more familiar "Trinity" representation of the Godhead. A triangle is commonly labeled *God*, with *Father* at the top, *Jesus* (or *Son*) on the lower left and *Spirit* on the lower right. My primary objection to this representation is the presumed hierarchical order when *Father* is always placed at the apex. Nor does it represent both the Unity of God and the unique Persons of the Godhead as Figure 2 attempts to do with the use of dashed lines. If the three Persons are represented *inside* the triangle, my objection is limited to what I said above. If, however, the three Persons are represented *outside* of the triangle, it becomes a representation of a modalistic God. (See Figure 5 below.)

Needless to say, most who use a drawing to represent God are not attempting to precisely represent all of His attributes. It is merely a graphic representation and we must be tolerant of that. Nonetheless, caution is in order. Many base their understanding of the Godhead on these quickly drawn illustrations.

---

[2] The identification of God as Elohim is plural in Hebrew. It is, however, probably a plural form recognizing majesty rather than number.

## Other views of the Godhead

Throughout the history of the Church, there have been numerous views of the Person of God. Within two hundred years of Jesus' life, there were debates and heresies regarding the Person of Christ resulting in various explanations of the Godhead.[3]

I cannot give a historical background of the different views of the Godhead in this short appendix. I am merely selecting several invalid ideas encountered in churches today. You can contrast them with the graphic representation of Figure 2. In all but Figure 8, their proponents would acknowledge that Jesus—and probably the Spirit as well—is God. Your own study of Scripture will help you determine the truth or error of each viewpoint.

## God is greater than the three Persons

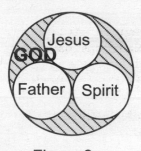

Figure 3

Figure 3 represents a view that God is something more than the three Persons, Father, Spirit, and Jesus. This is not typically a stated doctrinal position, but it may well be a misconception of many.

This viewpoint properly identifies the three equal Persons in the Godhead, and it has a basis of recognition of the Unity of the Godhead. However, it sees God as something more than the three Persons.

## A polytheistic God

I have stressed the Unity of God in order to avoid another potential misconception. God is not merely three Persons who all, by chance, are Eternal and Absolute. The Unity of God transcends the existence of the individual Persons. Figure 4 represents three, individual Gods in communication with each other (as represented by the arrows). We need

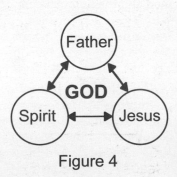

Figure 4

---

[3] For an excellent study of the numerous heresies in the early Church, see the book *Heresies*, by Harold O. J. Brown, Hendrickson Publishers, 1988.

to be careful that we do not distort what was depicted in Figure 2. God is not three equal—though distinct—deities.

This viewpoint properly identifies the three equal Persons in the Godhead, but it does not recognize the Unity of the Godhead.

### A Modalistic God

Modalism, an early heresy in the Church, described God as a single Being with three manifestations. That is, the single Being manifested Himself as the Father in the Old Testament. In the New Testament He took on a human form as Jesus in

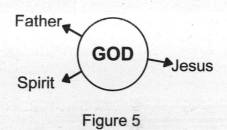

Figure 5

order to live as a man and pay the price of redemption. At Pentecost He appeared as the Spirit. A number of explanations have been attempted allowing the simultaneous presence of the Father and the Spirit at Jesus' baptism, etc. A surprising number of evangelicals today have a modified modalistic view of the Godhead.

This viewpoint properly identifies the Unity of the Godhead, but it denies the three distinct Persons of the Godhead.

### One Supreme God

In practice, the viewpoint most commonly held by evangelical Christians today is represented by either Figure 6a or Figure 6b. They see the Father as the Supreme God, and Jesus and the Spirit as lesser Gods. Though most would strongly object to the term *lesser God* when speaking of Jesus or the Spirit, they have no difficulty identifying the Father as the Supreme authority.

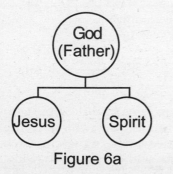

Figure 6a

Figure 6a represents one variation in which *God* is generally understood to be the *Father*. Leading to much confusion, Jesus and the Spirit are also called *God*, but are assigned lower rank.

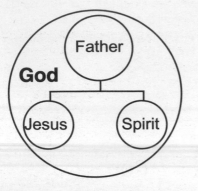

**Figure 6b**

Figure 6b represents a more complete understanding of the distinction between the corporate Unity of the Godhead and the Person of the Father. Nonetheless, the faulty hierarchical arrangement is maintained.

This viewpoint is usually depicted by an equilateral triangle.

The viewpoints of both Figure 6a and Figure 6b correctly identify all three Persons as being God. However, both arrangements must logically deny the Absolute nature of two Persons of the Godhead because the Father is placed above them as being pre-eminent. The convenience of the viewpoint of either Figure 6a or Figure 6b is its simple explanation of Jesus' statements that He is "under" the Father.

### A Gnostic God

In this viewpoint, God is depicted in a hierarchical arrangement. It varies little from the *Supreme God* viewpoint in Figure 6a other than its placement of the Spirit under Jesus' authority.

This viewpoint correctly identifies three Persons in the Godhead, but it does not recognize God's Unity because it denies the Absolute nature of all but the Father. However, with this viewpoint, there is superficially less difficulty reconciling Jesus' statement regarding His relationship with the Father, and the seemingly slight emphasis in Scripture on the Spirit's status as God.

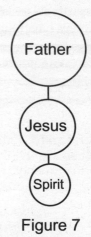

**Figure 7**

### A single God with a created son

The above depictions of God all portray Jesus (and the Spirit, to some degree) as being God. However, there are many who deny the deity of Jesus. It is impossible to adequately represent each viewpoint that denies the deity of Christ with a single drawing. However, any viewpoint denying the deity of Christ will contain the common element of a difference between the Absolute nature of the Father and all other created beings who differ in nature from Him. In some cases, the Spirit may be viewed as a power rather than a Person. For many, Jesus logically becomes, in a Gnostic sense, an intermediary between God and man. (That is, because Jesus is lower than God but higher than mankind, humans can communicate

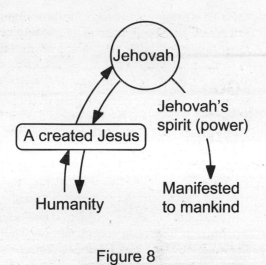

**Figure 8**

with him more easily than with God, or communicate with God through his agency. In a reciprocal arrangement, God communicates to humans through the agency of Jesus.) This view of God is represented in Figure 8.

This viewpoint properly identifies the Unity of God, but it denies the deity of either Jesus or the Spirit.

### "God" and "Father"

We often interchange *God* (or *Yahweh*) and *Father*. When we read passages such as "In the beginning God created the heavens and the earth," (Genesis 1:1 NASB) and "Thus says [Yahweh] 'It is I who made the earth, and created man upon it. I stretched out the heavens with My hands, and I ordained all their hosts,'" (Isaiah 45:11-12 NASB) we usually visualize the Father as the One being described or speaking.

If we interchange *God* and *Father*, we create complexity in a passage like Colossians 1:16 which says of Jesus,

For in Him all things were created, both in the heavens and on earth, visible and invisible, whether thrones or dominions or rulers or authorities—all things have been created through Him and for Him. (NASB)

If we would simply understand that unless the context specifies otherwise (Scripture does sometimes use *God the Father*), we must understand that the term *God* or *Yahweh* (or the capitalized *LORD* in

the Old Testament) means the corporate Godhead.  The Father  did
not create heaven and earth.  *God*, without specifying any  individual
Person of the Godhead, created all things.

Quoting these two passages using symbols rather  than  *God*,
*Yahweh*  or *Jesus* will  illustrate  what  has  just  been  said.   The  basic
symbol of Figure 2 without highlight  represents  *God*  (or  *Yahweh*).
However, when one Person of the Godhead is identified in  the  verse,
that Person will be highlighted  in  the  symbol.  By  using  the  symbol
from Figure 2, we will not minimize the Unity of God because all  are
present even when only one is highlighted. The position of the  names
*Father*,  *Spirit* and *Jesus* will  alternate  in  the  symbol  to  emphasize
the fact that there is no hierarchy in the Godhead.

Read the passages below and see if you can better visualize w h a t
Scripture is trying to communicate.  There is  no  discrepancy  between
the two reports.  The New Testament is merely adding precision  to
the Old Testament's statement.

In  the  beginning  created the heavens
and the earth.

Thus says  "It is I who made the earth, and

created man upon it.   I stretched out the heavens  with  My
hands, and I ordained all their hosts."

For in  all things were created, both in

the heavens and on earth,

visible and invisible, whether thrones or dominions

or rulers or authorities—all things have been created

through  and for

The New Testament often refers to the *Father*, *God*, and *Jesus* in the same verse. For example, 1 Thessalonians 1:1-2 says,

Paul and Silvanus and Timothy to the Church of the Thessalonians in God the Father and the Lord Jesus Christ: Grace to you and peace. We give thanks to God always for all of you.

These two verses would look like this using our symbols:

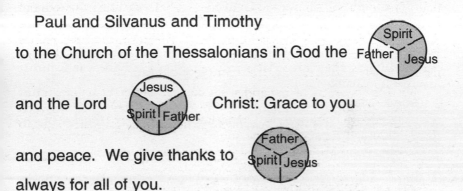

Paul and Silvanus and Timothy

to the Church of the Thessalonians in God the Father Jesus

and the Lord Jesus Spirit Father Christ: Grace to you

and peace. We give thanks to Father Spirit Jesus

always for all of you.

Space prevents carrying this any further, though we could also use a similar symbol for the Spirit. Hopefully, these graphics have represented something not easily communicated with words.

———————   •   ———————

# BIBLIOGRAPHY

All but one of the following books are biographies rather than devotional studies. Faith is often better *modeled* than *described*. The more pertinent books are identified with a bullet (•) and the most highly recommended with a double bullet (••).

There are three women mentioned in the following books who merit special attention. Each made a great contribution to her husband's ministry, and was in her own right a woman of great faith and ability. They are Mary Müller, Maria Taylor, and Biddy (Gertrude) Chambers.

••*George Müller of Bristol, His Life of Prayer and Faith*, A.T. Pierson, Kregel Publications, Grand Rapids MI, 1999 (reprint of the 1899 edition), 375 pages. As the sub-title suggests, this is an excellent book describing Müller's faith and prayer life.

•*George Müller, Delighted in God!* Roger Steer, Harold Shaw Publishers, Wheaton IL, 1981, 320 pages. This book is primarily concerned with the events of the Müllers' lives, though it also gives adequate insight into George Müller's prayer life and faith.

*George Müller on Faith, a 30-day Devotional Treasury*, Lance Wubbels, editor, Emerald Books, Lynnwood WA, 1998, 62 pages. This is a short book of devotional readings collected from Müller's writings.

••*J. Hudson Taylor, God's Man in China*, Dr. and Mrs. Howard Taylor, Moody Press, Chicago IL, 1977, 366 pages. This book is out of print, but is worth searching for. Of the books in this bibliography, it best describes Taylor's life of faith. It also gives the best account of Taylor's wife, Maria, as a woman of faith.

•*Hudson Taylor's Spiritual Secret*, Dr. and Mrs. Howard Taylor, Moody Press, Chicago IL, 1989, 256 pages. This book describes Hudson Taylor's experience of finding *resting* faith. It is an interesting study of a man who had long practiced *acting* faith, and then came to understand *resting* faith.

•*J. Hudson Taylor, A Man in Christ*, Roger Steer, OMF Books, Littleton CO, 1990 and 1993, 300 pages. This book gives good insight into Taylor's life. Taylor's faith is portrayed through his action.

•*John Hyde, Man of Faith,* (formerly titled, *Praying Hyde*) Francis McGaw, Bethany House Publishers, Minneapolis MN, 68 pages. This short book will leave a deep impression of the cost and effectiveness of total commitment to prayer. It may be out of print but is well worth reading.

•*Mountain Rain, A Biography of James O. Fraser,* Eileen Fraser Crossman, Harold Shaw Publishers, 1994, 246 pages. This book written by J.O. Fraser's daughter very adequately describes his life of prayer and faith.

•*Behind the Ranges, The Life-Changing Story of J.O. Fraser,* Geraldine Taylor, OMF Books, Littleton CO, 1944 and 1998, 300 pages. In the early 1900s, J.O. Fraser went to a remote area of China to work with an illiterate tribe untouched by the Gospel. This is an excellent book recounting Fraser's prayer and faith as he sought to win these people for Christ.

*The Prayer of Faith,* J.O. Fraser, OMF Books, Littleton CO, 1995, 29 pages. The material in this book is excerpted from *Behind the Ranges*. It is an interesting study on the prayer of faith.

••*Oswald Chambers, Abandoned to God,* David McCasland, Discovery House Publishers, Grand Rapids MI, 1993, 336 pages. This book gives good insight into the internal struggle involved in full commitment to Christ. The story of Chambers' wife, Biddy, is as compelling as that of Oswald Chambers himself.

•*Rees Howells, Intercessor,* Norman Grubb, Christian Literature Crusade, Fort Washington PA, 1952 and 1997, 263 pages. This book will certainly make the non-charismatic reader uncomfortable. However, it is an excellent book in its portrayal of the high cost of intercessory prayer.

••*God Crucified, Monotheism and Christology in the New Testament,* Richard Bauckham, William B. Eerdmans Publishing Company, Grand Rapids MI, 1998, 79 pages. This is the only non-biographical book cited in this appendix. However, this is an excellent book, giving important insights into the deity of Christ.

*William Carey, The Father of Modern Missions,* Basil Miller, Bethany House Publishers, Minneapolis MN, 1980, 152 pages.

## WORD RESOURCES, Inc.

Word Resources, Inc. is a privately-owned publishing company. Its primary purpose is the publication of books and tracts written for Jehovah's Witness readers. This is a subsidized ministry; we will never profit from book distribution. In order to encourage wide distribution, published material is not copyright protected.

No one wants to read books in which their beliefs are ridiculed and their church is harshly criticized. Even though it is appropriate to hold both ourselves and others to a high standard of biblical integrity, it is entirely inappropriate to present the truth of Scripture abrasively.

Word Resources publishes books that are historically and biblically accurate, while using terminology and reference sources familiar to the Jehovah's Witness reader. The tone of the books is always kind and respectful.

Our web site provides downloadable books discussing critical issues for Witness readers. The Internet is a valuable ministry tool. Contrary to what they might say, Jehovah's Witnesses are essentially prevented from reading books that are not published by the Watch Tower Society. In the privacy of their homes, however, some may access downloadable books from our web site.

*When you come into contact with Witnesses, let them know of the web site address.* (Send a request for "business cards" and a stamped, self-addressed envelope and we will send you a small supply of **www.tetragrammaton.org** cards you can give to Witnesses at your door. Free offer good while supplies last.) Do not be discouraged if they hand the card back to you. Because *Tetragrammaton* is a familiar word to them, they will remember the web site address.

Visit our web site in order to familiarize yourself with our downloadable and published books.

## www.tetragrammaton.org

**Word Resources, Inc.**
P.O. Box 301294
Portland, Oregon  97294-9294
USA

# DO YOU HAVE FRIENDS OR FAMILY MEMBERS WHO ARE JEHOVAH'S WITNESSES?

The Watch Tower Society teaches that the New Testament authors wrote the Hebrew name of God (with the Hebrew characters יהוה—YHWH) 237 times in the original New Testament. Based on this claim, their *New World Translation* Bible uses *Jehovah* rather than *Lord* 237 times in their New Testament. This alteration shifts the emphasis of deity away from Christ in many critical verses.

Word Resources, Inc. publishes literature which substantiates that the original New Testament writers used the Greek word for *Lord* rather than the Hebrew name of God. This topic is vital to all Jehovah's Witnesses because the use of *Lord* in many verses confirms the New Testament writers' claim that Jesus is truly God.

Printed material is one avenue of presenting the Gospel when you are prevented from speaking. These materials are written with respect and understanding of the Jehovah's Witness reader.

We can direct-mail a copy of these materials to anyone you designate. We generally send two booklets and one tract, using separate mailings. The envelope will not identify you as the sender unless you want to include your return address. If you wish, we will also send you a return letter letting you know when the materials were sent. We do not keep any addresses on record after the mailings.

If you have not personally seen the material, we suggest that you first order copies for yourself or carefully review it on our web site **www.tetragrammaton.org.** (You may simultaneously order a copy for yourself and someone else by using two mailing labels. See our web site for other materials that are also for sale.)

We generally mail the material in the following sequence. (We will substitute or delete titles if our stock is low.)

1. *A Field Service Encounter*—a 60-page booklet telling the story of Mike, a young Witness who faces a dilemma in his field service activity. (*Field service* is their work of literature distribution.) In searching for his answer, Mike discovers the lack of manuscript evidence for the Hebrew name of God in the original New Testament writings.

2. *The Tetragrammaton is Essential to Your Faith*—a tract that explains the consequences of the textual alteration to the faith of one relying on the *New World Translation.*

3. *The Divine Name in the New World Translation*—a 70-page booklet describing the lack of evidence for the *New World Translation*'s use of *Jehovah* in their New Testament.

If you are placing more than one order, **photocopy the order form below for each order and check the appropriate boxes for that order.** Make checks payable to Word Resources and mail to:

WORD RESOURCES, Inc.
P.O. Box 301294
Portland, OR 97294-9294

$8.00 includes the cost of items 1, 2, and 3 above, plus postage. If you make multiple orders, *enclose the full amount for all orders.*

Use the order form below. The address label will be affixed to the package. (Note: the handwriting on the order form will be seen by the recipient. If you prefer to remain anonymous, you may want to type the address.) Make photocopies for each additional order. Use one address label (with checked order boxes) for each order.

- - - - -✂- - - - - - Send one order form for each order- - - - - - - - - - - -

❑ This order is for a Jehovah's Witness reader. (Each item will be mailed individually.)

❑ This order is for my own use. (All items will be sent in one envelope.)

❑ Please send a verification notice to me when the material is sent to my Jehovah's Witness family member or friend. (Note: you must include your personal mailing address on a separate piece of paper.)

If the address below is that of a Jehovah's Witness to whom you wish literature sent, *add your return address (you may use a label) only if you want to be identified to the one receiving the literature.*

Name_____

Address_____

_____

## DO YOU HAVE FRIENDS OR FAMILY MEMBERS WHO ARE JEHOVAH'S WITNESSES?

The Watch Tower Society teaches that the New Testament authors wrote the Hebrew name of God (with the Hebrew characters יהוה—YHWH) 237 times in the original New Testament. Based on this claim, their *New World Translation* Bible uses *Jehovah* rather than *Lord* 237 times in their New Testament. This alteration shifts the emphasis of deity away from Christ in many critical verses.

Word Resources, Inc. publishes literature which substantiates that the original New Testament writers used the Greek word for *Lord* rather than the Hebrew name of God. This topic is vital to all Jehovah's Witnesses because the use of *Lord* in many verses confirms the New Testament writers' claim that Jesus is truly God.

Printed material is one avenue of presenting the Gospel when you are prevented from speaking. These materials are written with respect and understanding of the Jehovah's Witness reader.

We can direct mail a copy of these materials to anyone you designate. We generally send two booklets and one tract, using separate mailings. The envelope will not identify you as the sender unless you want to include your return address. If you wish, we will also send you a return letter letting you know when the materials were sent. We do not keep any addresses on record after the mailings.

If you have not personally seen the material, we suggest that you first order copies for yourself or carefully review it on our web site **www.tetragrammaton.org**. (You may simultaneously order a copy for yourself and someone else by using two mailing labels. See our web site for other materials that are also for sale.)

We generally mail the material in the following sequence. (We will substitute or delete titles if our stock is low.)

4. *A Field Service Encounter*—a 60-page booklet telling the story of Mike, a young Witness who faces a dilemma in his field service activity. (*Field service* is their work of literature distribution.) In searching for his answer, Mike discovers the lack of manuscript evidence for the Hebrew name of God in the original New Testament writings.

5. *The Tetragrammaton is Essential to Your Faith*—a tract that explains the consequences of the textual alteration to the faith of one relying on the *New World Translation*.

6. *The Divine Name in the New World Translation*—a 70-page booklet describing the lack of evidence for the *New World Translation*'s use of *Jehovah* in their New Testament.

If you are placing more than one order, **photocopy the order form below for each order and check the appropriate boxes for that order.** Make checks payable to Word Resources and mail to:

WORD RESOURCES, Inc.
P.O. Box 301294
Portland, OR 97294-9294

$8.00 includes the cost of items 1, 2, and 3 above, plus postage. If you make multiple orders, *enclose the full amount for all orders.*

Use the order form below. The address label will be affixed to the package. (Note: the handwriting on the order form will be seen by the recipient. If you prefer to remain anonymous, you may want to type the address.) Make photocopies for each additional order. Use one address label (with checked order boxes) for each order.

- - - - -✂- - - - - - Send one order form for each order- - - - - - - - - - - -

❏ This order is for a Jehovah's Witness reader. (Each item will be mailed individually.)

❏ This order is for my own use. (All items will be sent in one envelope.)

❏ Please send a verification notice to me when the material is sent to my Jehovah's Witness family member or friend. (Note: you must include your personal mailing address on a separate piece of paper.)

If the address below is that of a Jehovah's Witness to whom you wish literature sent, *add your return address (you may use a label) only if you want to be identified to the one receiving the literature.*

Name_____

Address_____

_____